CONTENTS

ACKNOWLEDGMENTS

I gratefully acknowledge the generous assistance of the following, who shared quilts, photographs, and research information:

Martha Ahern, Back Street Designs, Cuesta Benberry, Barbara Brackman, John Bradley, Karey Bresenhan, Chester County Historical Society, Jean Christensen, Cumberland County Historical Society, Nancy and Dick Dice, Dorling, Kindersley, Ltd., Luella Doss, E. P. Dutton, Nancy Eisen, Adabelle Gardner, Ruth Hare Ghormley, Arlene B. Giegling, Maxine Gill, Goschenhoppen Historians, Inc., Groves Publishing, Suzanne Hammond, Joseph and Joan Hannum, Pat Hedwall, Historical Society of Montgomery County, Felicia Holtzinger, Jeana Kimball, Martha Kinsey, Grace Koenig, Marsha McCloskey, Mercer Museum, Marjorie Meyers, Sara Nephew, Roxana Orr, Pat Orslund, Nancy Lee Papay, Bets Ramsey, Nancy Roan, Elly Sienkiewicz, Judith Slicer, Sharon Stanley, Stearns Technical Textiles, Nadene Stephenson, Ann Stohl, Marion Strode, Jean Pringle Swanson, Helen L. Thompson, Ann Troianello, Nancyann Twelker, Tirza Williams, Winthethur Museum, Sandra Wolf, Virginia Wolfe, Yakima Valley Museum, Sharon Yenter, and Lois Zaremba.

A special thank you to:

Freda Smith, Bev Payne, Judy Eide, and Jean Fries and her quilting service, for quilting my tops; Joan Duranceau, Judy Eide, Paula Erickson, Marta Estes, Shirley Gundlach, Joan Hanson, Sue von Jentzen, Marsha McCloskey, Leanne Ober, Carolann Palmer, Beverly Payne, Suzette Pearson, Judy Pollard, Carol Porter, Nadene Stephenson, Nancy Sweeney, and Ferol Yust for pattern testing;

Julie Lampson and Kristy Smith for their research assistance;

Marion Shelton for her competent assistance and organization of the many details.

PHOTO CREDITS

Borge B. Andersen — Nos. 28, 29, 39, 47, 61

George Fistrovich — No. 18

Skip Howard Photos — Nos. 2, 6, 7, 8, 9, 16, 19, 20, 22, 25, 26, 27, 56

Brent Kane — Nos. 21, 23, 24, 30, 31, 32, 33, 34, 35, 36, 37, 38, 41, 42, 43, 44, 48, 49, 50, 51, 52, 53, 54, 55, 57, 58, 60, 64, 65, 66, 67, 68, 69, 70

Carl Murray — Nos. 1, 11, 15, 45, 59, 63

Brian McNeill — Nos. 13, 14

Zintgraff — No. 62

THREADS *of* TIME
Nancy J. Martin

That Patchwork Place ®

CREDITS

Illustration and Graphics . . . . Stephanie Benson
Text and Cover Design . . . . Judy Petry
Editor . . . . Liz McGehee

Threads of Time©
©1990 by Nancy J. Martin
That Patchwork Place, Inc., PO Box 118, Bothell, WA
98041-0118.

Printed in the Republic of Korea
97 96 95 94 93 92 91 90   6 5 4 3 2 1

Library of Congress Cataloging-in-Publication Data

Martin, Nancy J.
  Threads of Time/Nancy J. Martin
    p.   cm.
    Includes bibliographical references.
    ISBN 0-943574-66-8 :   —ISBN 0-943574-65-X (soft) :
    1. Quilting—Patterns.   2. Quilting—United States—
History.   3. Patchwork—Patterns.   I. Title.
TT835.M3834   1990   89-40800
746.9′7′0973—dc20   CIP

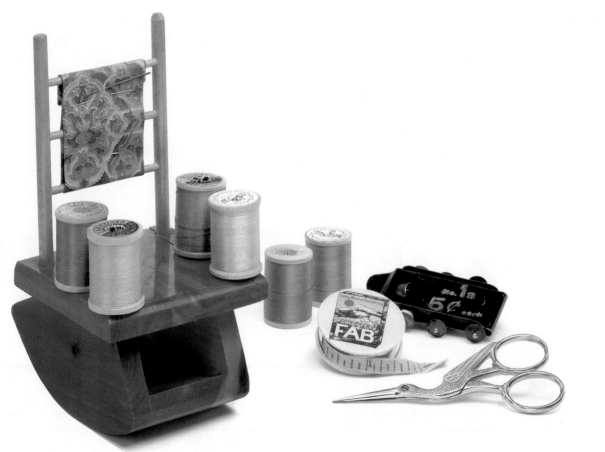

THREADS *of* TIME

INTRODUCTION

My interest in quilt history began in 1984, when I started to collect and document antique quilts. As a result, I was prompted to write *Pieces of the Past,* a pictorial overview of quiltmaking history between 1750 and 1940. Covering almost two hundred years of quilt history in a specified number of pages dictated a brief presentation and left little room for the colorful narratives that tell us so much about quiltmakers' lives.

Nonetheless, the response to *Pieces of the Past* was overwhelming. I had awakened an interest in many quilters and encouraged others to seek out the documentation of their quilts. I had also aroused my own interest. I continued to avidly collect quilts and was quite fortunate in researching and documenting many of these quilts. Association with quilt scholars and historians through the American Quilt Study Group fostered a continual exchange of information and added to my research. As I uncovered interesting stories and facts, there came a familiar urge to write and share this information, to continue the *Threads of Time.*

Threads of Time takes an in-depth look at several quilting styles or types of quilts. In most cases, but not all, these quilts are arranged in a loose chronological sequence. As most quiltmakers know, rarely is one type of quilt made to the exclusion of all others. The popularity of particular quilt types often overlaps others, while some enjoy concurrent interest. But, there are periods in quiltmaking history where trends toward a specific quilt type are evident. Indeed, the short span of years and the intensity with which some quilts were made might classify them as a fad.

The exception to this loose chronology is the period from 1910–1940, the period of the first quilt revival through the thirties. This period did not produce a particular style of quilt, but an eclectic gathering of all quilt types, having mainly in common the myriad of gay pastel fabrics that were available. Since this period is within our recent past, much information is known and available. It is difficult for the writer to choose which of these facts to include, since much of our quiltmaking heritage today was influenced by this period of time.

My own private quilt collection revealed several types of quilts on which very little research has been done, particularly the strippy style I found in Pennsylvania. As a quiltmaker, I became interested in recreating quilts made in the strippy style. I have included directions for making several quilts whose styles are no longer popular: the strippy, chintz medallion, and a variation of Sunshine and Shadows.

A collection of patchwork and appliqué patterns, along with a description of basic quiltmaking techniques for those preferring a traditional approach, is included. Several classic quilts, done in new Template-Free™ techniques, are also presented.

A quilt is far more than three layers of materials held together by meticulous stitches. For many quilters, it is the thread that connects them to others, whether in day-to-day activities or to stitchers of past generations. Quilts have always offered women the opportunity to experiment with new colors, designs, and styles. *Threads of Time* will connect you to past stitchers and allow you to recreate a style from a past era, experiment with new techniques, or utilize a traditional pattern.

Chapter 1

IN THE ENGLISH STYLE

QUILTS CROSS THE ATLANTIC

Our early American ancestors brought the quilting styles of their homeland to the New World. Quilting was part of the Englishwoman's repertoire of skillful needlework, but before 1700, quilting was used mostly on whole-cloth quilts or to outline crewel work on bed hangings. Margaret E. White of the Newark Museum writes, "Their story [quilts] begins with the first settlers of New England and New Amsterdam for the introduction of patchwork into America is credited to the thrifty English and Dutch colonists."[1]

During the eighteenth and nineteenth century, two styles of quilting developed in England: mosaic (patchwork) and appliquéd work (appliqué). The mosaic patchwork was often sewn to papers, then joined together. Indeed, the technique is referred to as English paper piecing and is still frequently used today. Directions for this technique are found on page 170.

Patterns and fabric traveled in both directions across the Atlantic. "By 1850, fabric production in the United States was growing rapidly; however, much of the cloth used by Americans was still made abroad. It is important to note that, during the eighteenth and most of the nineteenth centuries, American trade in foreign textiles was of economic importance similar to trade in steel or oil today."[2]

Many of the fabrics seen in the early quilts of the United States are of English origin. These were the "painted calicoes" or "chints" first imported from India in the seventeenth century. The definition of chintz has changed over the years. In the early 1800s, chintz was a tightly woven cotton fabric, usually printed with a large-scale print and often, but not always, containing a glazed finish. Chintz was used for both furnishings and clothing, with the clothing fabrics having a smaller-scale print. Women on both sides of the Atlantic were entranced by these gaily colored cottons for both their dressmaking and quiltmaking (since dressmaking scraps often found their way into patchwork quilts).

English textile manufacturers sought to ban the import of these cheap Indian calicoes and chintzes, which were highly prized over the wool and linen produced domestically. However, restricting the import of these chintzes only served to make them more popular and to raise the prices of "charming chintz." The popularity of these Indian calicoes and chintzes influenced English textile manufacturing in the years that followed. "They are typical not only of the traditional Indian native painted calicoes, but they can be recognized as the inspiration of the many floral and leaf designs printed in England during the next hundred years."[3]

Early textile manufacturing in England used wood blocks to print the designs on fabric until 1752, when the copper-plate process first used in Ireland was adopted. Fabrics manufactured by the copper-plate process were finer and more detailed, showing the close engraving lines of the pattern. Both the green and yellow prints found in the Star of Bethlehem (no. 1) show the detail achieved using copper-plate fabric printing.

Advances in fabric, such as the developing of a single process for printing solid green in 1809 and printing by mechanical rollers, which was in general use by 1815, lowered the price of English textiles.

However, chintz was still an expensive fabric. Even at the height of chintz's popularity, few quilts were made from it, not only because of its high price but also because it was in short supply. As chintz became more available, the price dropped, but never as low as the calicoes.

Chintz quilts were made as "best" quilts and brought out only on special occasions. Few quilts were made entirely from chintz, but many quilts incorporated the scraps from clothing or furnishings. "In 1800 cottons were cheap to buy; 'printed cottons' were two shillings a yard and a few years later the 'new printed chintzes' could be bought for seven or eight shillings a yard according to quality."[4]

Many patchwork patterns were shared with family and friends across the sea. Averil Colby attributes their development to England but allows that patterns could travel both ways: "So many of the American patterns are exactly identical with a number which are traditional in the Northern Counties of England that it is reasonable to think that the original patterns first went out from Durham, Cumberland, Northumberland, and Westmorland. Some of the earlier quilts [American] at the beginning of the nineteenth century contain English textiles which are of the same design as the chintzes used in patchwork made in this country at the same time. No doubt many of the patchwork patterns (as well as the quilting ones) traveled back across the Atlantic to the country of their origin with the addition of local and topical variations in name and design, and also new patterns which had grown out of the old; a needlework pattern is often a family heirloom and many such must have made the journey across the sea."[5]

Star of Bethlehem

The Star of Bethlehem was a quilt pattern popular in both American and English patchwork in the late 1700s. According to the Shelburne Museum catalog, "This quilt design radiating from a small centered star out to the edges of the quilt was named in honor of, and to commemorate, the light with its far-reaching brightness that shone over the stable the night of Christ's birth."[6]

Several quilts made from this pattern of both British and American origin are in the collection of the Victoria and Albert Museum in London. In America, this star design was often given regional names such as Rising Star, Rising Sun, Lone Star, Blazing Star, and Lone Star of Texas.

Despite their association with America, large star quilts are not exclusive to this country, as British examples have been traced back as far as the late eighteenth century. A search of museum catalogs reveals that many star quilts in their collections, listed under various names, are quite large in size. The largest in the Victoria and Albert collection, listed

under the name Star of Bethlehem, is 106 by 110 inches, while several listed in the collection of the Shelburne Museum in Vermont are at least 110 by 110 inches. Most of the old beds were quite high, some requiring steps to enter them. Even so, quilts this large must have hung all the way to the floor. Since most of the early beds were poster beds, it is interesting that there are no corner cutouts. Mrs. Florence Peto offers an ingenious and simple explanation for the use of these large quilts. "In the Paul Revere house in Boston there was but one sleeping room for Revere, his wife, and their twelve children. The youngest child probably slept with its parents while the others slept in the trundle bed and on pallets laid on the floor. In the morning the pallets and their bedding together with that of the trundle bed was placed on the parents' bed, making a mound so high that a large quilt was necessary to cover it."[7]

Examining the fabrics and design used in most of these Star of Bethlehem quilts, I wonder if they weren't "best quilts" brought out only for special occasions. Thus, the maker didn't have to be practical about the size and could create a true masterpiece as large as she desired.

Ruby McKim writes about the pattern: "Lone Star, sometimes called 'Star of the East' or 'Star of Bethlehem,' is one of the more ambitious projects in quilt making, and yet the result is so effective that many have completed coverlets of this design. In making any quilt, one should think of the top as a whole; in making a Lone Star it is imperative. . . . For quilting, we suggest a large Rising Sun to fill in the squares and half squares."[8]

Yet, among the Pennsylvania Dutch (more accurately referred to as Pennsylvania Deutsch or German) community, the quilt was called Rising Sun. In response to the question "What is a Rising Sun?," posed to local quiltmakers in the Goschenhoppen (Pennsylvania) region as part of an oral research project done by Nancy Roan and Ellen Gehret, they received the following information:

"My grandmother made these big Rising Sun quilts, the real kind. She laid them things all on the floor, and then you pick 'em up and put them in a straight [line], and that I did for her. She just went to the sewing machine and sewed it together, and it came out perfect. Well, it's a great big star, the whole quilt. It's big! And then in four corners you had a smaller star. That was the original quilt. And that's called Rising Sun."[9]

The Star of Bethlehem Quilt shown in no. 1

1. Star of Bethlehem, c. 1835,
New England, 110 x 120 inches,
appliquéd and pieced cottons.
(Collection of Nancy J. Martin)

consists of a large central pieced star, surrounded by smaller stars. Both the fabrics used and the quilt's large size suggest a New England origin of about 1835. In addition to the interesting copper-plate printed fabrics used in the quilt, one also finds "rainbow fabric." This is fabric printed in variegated shades of a color and is frequently found in Baltimore Album quilts. The eight stars used in the corner and triangular sections surrounding the central star are made of two or three fabrics and appliquéd to the white fabric. Pieced stars made from three of the fabrics form the next border. On what is presumably the top of the quilt, there is a single row of these stars, while a double row of stars is found on the remaining three sides. A half diamond or pyramid design with an interesting corner configuration forms the outermost border.

The quilt has a coarse muslin backing, and the back of the quilt is turned to the front for the edge finishing. Elaborate quilting in feather designs fills the open areas of the quilt. All of the star designs, including the large center star, have quilting inside of each diamond shape.

TUMBLING BLOCKS

The Tumbling Blocks pattern was also known by many names on both sides of the Atlantic. In America, it was also referred to as the Box Pattern, Variegated Diamonds, Shifting Cubes, Baby's Blocks, Building Blocks, Box upon Box, Cubework, Golden Cubes, Jacob's Ladder, Stairstep Quilt, Disappearing Blocks, Stairs of Illusion, Steps to the Altar, and the English T Box.

In England, we find this design also referred to as

2. Tumbling Blocks, c. 1870,
New Hampshire, 78½ x 81
inches, pieced cottons. (Collection
of Nancy J. Martin)

Reversible Box, Box and Diamond, or The Heavenly Steps. The earliest example found was made in 1852.[10]

Because of the many bias edges and angled seams, this quilt is usually done in the English paper-piecing method (see page 170).

The Tumbling Blocks quilt shown in no. 2 contains three equally sized diamond units. These units fit together to give a trompe l'oeil effect of three-dimensional boxes and are assembled in the English paper-piecing method. The boxes appear to be stacked in vertical rows with an attempt to consistently use the same fabric for the box side. The prints used in the other two diamond units alternate. Often, these two prints are combined for several rows, with only the fabric used for the box side changing in each row, making it the dominant element in the design.

The unknown quiltmaker who made this quilt in New Hampshire around 1870 was quite artistic in her fabric placement. The rows of boxes along the sides of the quilt and along the lower edge are much darker in color. Thus, there is a color gradation from dark to light, resulting in a deeper border to hang over the edge of the mattress. A contrasting five-inch-wide border was added to the top edge to give this quilt the necessary length. This quilt was made for a four-poster bed, so the quilter left cutouts in each corner

3. English Wedding Quilt, 1850, Northumberland, England, pieced cottons. (Photo courtesy Dorling, Kindersley, Ltd., London)

to accommodate the bedposts. A coarse muslin was used for the backing, and the quilt was bound with a pink-and-white print. The quilt is finely quilted inside of each diamond shape.

CHINTZ MEDALLION QUILTS

Printed chintz quilts were popular on both sides of the Atlantic with eighteenth and nineteenth century quilters. Framed center, center medallion, or framed medallion quilts were made in England during the late eighteenth century. As the severity of life in the American colonies decreased, wives of prospering colonists began to adopt this style of quilt.

The term "medallion quilt" refers to a quilt featuring a central motif, surrounded by a series of borders. The medallion-style quilt was often chosen to feature a particular chintz print or panel in the center. Smaller pieces of chintz fabric, scraps from dressmaking or salesmen's sample books, were sometimes used in the surrounding squares and borders.

The English Wedding Quilt in no. 3, made by Annie Heslop of Northumberland, England, in 1850, features a lovely chintz fabric in the center. It is surrounded by multicolor chintz squares from a sample book and a brown print border. Since this was a wedding quilt, a true lover's knot design was elaborately quilted in the center square.

Annie Heslop's wedding quilt is a variation of the medallion style and is unusual in the use of its diagonal setting. The simple design, using large pieces of fabric, is a good choice for these busy chintz prints.

Quilts such as this one served as samplers for the various chintz fabrics available. Contemporary quilters may enjoy using this style of quilt to showcase some of their favorite fabrics, chintz or otherwise. Directions

4. English Medallion Quilt, 1820-1830,
England, 98 x 104 inches, pieced cottons.
(Photo courtesy E. P. Dutton)

for making this type of chintz medallion quilt are found on page 115.

The chintz medallion quilt shown in no. 4 is more typical of the style made in England during the late eighteenth century. Found in New York State, this quilt features a center block of tiny patchwork pieces, framed by a narrow border of dark fabric. The ensuing rows of borders are mainly squares placed on the diagonal, although there is also a pyramid border, a plain border of squares, and a wide chintz border. Each pieced border is anchored in the corners by a different patchwork block.

Medallion quilts of this type were often developed as they were sewn, rather than planned in advance. Several of the pieced borders shown in this quilt are very randomly matched, suggesting they were cut to fit as the quilt was being constructed.

The most striking border in this quilt is the outer border, which features a wide band of chintz panels. This large-scale print reflects the type of fabric used in that day for furnishings and draperies, which were often printed with idealized scenes of frolicking country folk. It is similar to the "Toile de Jouy" patterns popularized in France.

STRIPPY QUILTS

Originating in northeast England, the strippy quilt is the simplest type of patchwork. Long lengths or strips of fabric are cut to the size of the quilt, pieced together, and embellished with elaborate quilting. Indeed, early English versions were usually done in solid-color fabric to show off the detailed quilting designs. The quilt pictured in no. 5 is an excellent example. It was made in 1870 by Elizabeth Womphrey in Wallsend, England.

"The strip quilt and the whole cloth quilt were the

*5. English Strippy Quilt, 1870,
Wallsend, England, pieced
cottons. (Photo courtesy Dorling,
Kindersley, Ltd., London)*

preferred 'canvas' on which most quilters of Wales, Durham, and Northumberland chose to work. Quilting in their minds was a much higher art than piecing, and although they changed their ideas about color and cloth . . . they stayed true to the original format. Strip quilts in Turkey red and white were a traditional combination in both Durham and Northumberland and obviously one which had certain advantages. It was easier to work patterns in long continuous strips than to deal with a central motif; and one strip could be marked at a time as the quilt was unrolled in the frame. Strip quilts were also made in Wales, though often in wool and in different color combinations. And in the Isle of Man the striped tops were made in two colors—dark blue, red, and black or green being the preferred choices."[11]

Another variation of the strippy quilt featured vertical panels of patchwork alternating with solid or printed cottons. This version is found in both the north counties of England from the late 1700s on and also in the mid-1800s in America. Averil Colby, in her book *Patchwork,* illustrates two versions made in County Durham. The first design consists of long triangles attached to a center strip to form the Tree Everlasting pattern. It was made from lavender and primrose dress cottons. The second is a strip quilt made with a zigzag design of purple and creamy buff printed cottons done in the late nineteenth century. Colby cites that "the North Country 'strippies' are simpler and do not contain more than one pattern in the patchwork of a quilt. A favorite with North Country workers is the bellows pattern, others prefer a pattern with stars in colored print with wide stripes between the rows."[12]

Early strippy designs can be found in Pennsylvania, where there was a great concentration of immigrants from Wales and northern England. In fact, William Penn sold 20,000 acres of his original purchase to the Free Society of Traders, a Welsh colonization company, which settled what is now part of Delaware, Chester, and Montgomery counties. This area continued to attract immigrants from Wales and northern England.

These strippy quilts were made from lengths of printed fabric (no. 6), so the quilting stitches were not as evident. Since this style could be pieced together quickly, the strippy quilt was most often made as a utility quilt for everyday use. Those who enjoyed elaborate quilting would continue to embellish their work. These quilts often contained the simple Four Patch or Ninepatch blocks, as in no. 7.

7. *Striped Strippy, c. 1870, origin unknown, 80 x 96 inches, pieced cottons. (Collection of Nancy J. Martin)*

6. *Pennsylvania Strippy, c. 1860, Berks County, Pennsylvania, 82 x 85 inches, pieced cottons. (Collection of Nancy J. Martin)*

Tirza Williams' family quilt (no. 8) is an excellent example of one of these utility quilts. Her great-grandmother, Christine Wolfgang, married William Clauser on 19 March 1864. She was a young bride and so was her daughter Loretta Clauser, who married Daniel Weller on 27 October 1883. This mother-and-daughter pair often quilted together, making many utility quilts for the cold Pennsylvania winters.

The Clauser and Weller families lived near Boyertown, Berks County, Pennsylvania, where quilting was a popular activity. According to oral resources in the Goschenhoppen area, both fabrics and printed patterns

were available. "Joel Weller used to have a store in Boyertown to buy materials. We got there by trolley." [13]

"My grandmother always quilted, my mother's mother, and she collected all the patterns from the newspapers as they came out . . . from the *Boyertown Democrat* or whatever it was called and the Reading papers. She just took the clippings out of the newspaper, and she pieced a block. She didn't send for the patterns." [14]

The quilt is made from simple Four-Patch units alternated with print squares for the strips. These strips alternate with striped fabric, which was often used in a strippy quilt (see no. 7). The backing is pieced from two different black-and-white prints, probably dress or waist (blouse) scraps. These small black-and-white prints were probably produced at the Eddystone Manufacturing Company in Chester, Pennsylvania. It was one of the largest American print works, printing 24,000 pieces of fabric each week. The Company, also know as Simpson Print Works, specialized in "mourning and Fancy Prints." Salesman sample sheets also are labeled "Silver Greys" and indicate that these fabrics were produced between 1880 and 1900. [15]

The front edges are turned to the back, a common

10. *Album-Patch Strippy, 1844,*
Montgomery County,
Pennsylvania, 102½ x 111½
inches, pieced cottons. (Collection
of Mercer Museum)

As mentioned in the previous chapter, chintz fabrics were popular in both England and America. Decorative panels were printed in England from 1810 to 1816. The panels featured varying shapes surrounded by a decorated border. "The factories produced special chintz borders to match those round panels which were put into 'framed' quilts or as a final border." [16]

Two different chintz borders are effectively used in the quilt shown in no. 10. This signature quilt was made by two sisters, Mary C. and Lydia Ann Walton of Horsham, Montgomery County, Pennsylvania. Each

Album block contains a signature and a date: 1843, 1844, or 1845. Lydia Ann was born 27 July 1827 to Silas and Priscilla Walton. They were members of the Religious Society of Friends and attended the Gwynedd Meeting. On 14 February 1850, at the age of 22, Lydia married Charles Conrad, son of John and Sarah Conrad of Whitpain, Montgomery County, Pennsylvania, at the home of her parents. Lydia and Charles had ten children, and Charles made a living through farming.

Mary Walton was Lydia's younger sister and was born 17 July 1830. At the age of 29, Mary married Isaac

Conrad, son of John and Sarah of Whitmarsh, Montgomery County, Pennsylvania, on 6 April 1854, also at her parents' home. Mary and Isaac had three children and named the middle child for Mary's sister Lydia. The marriage certificates of the Gwynedd meeting (no. 399 for Lydia and no. 412 for Mary) list all the guests present. None of the names correspond to the names signed on the quilt.

This signature quilt was made five to seven years prior to Lydia's marriage and nine to eleven years before Mary's marriage, so it is unlikely the quilt was made as a bridal quilt, although this design was often made for "a gift for a bride-to-be. A group of friends would get together and each would piece a block and embroider her name on it. Then, of course, they would all come to the quilting bee, and the result, while not exactly a bride's shower, was something to store for a rainy day."[17] Lydia Walton was seventeen when she made her signature block, and Mary would have been fourteen. When the 1850 census was taken five years later, several of the quilt's signers were still residing in Montgomery County. Upon checking the census, I found their names and ages when they signed the blocks: Hannah Willard (innkeeper), 51; Jane Kenderdine, 21; Tacy Lukens, 25; Adaline Harper, 25; Elizabeth Kenderdine, 23; Martha Shoemaker, 16; Sarah Shoemaker, 25; Jane S. Hallowell, 14; and Ann C. Hobensack, 18.

Not all of the people who signed the quilt were from Montgomery County. Quite a few were from Chester County or Philadelphia. Not all the signers were female. The quilt also bears the names of Dr. David Hutcherson, 1845; John D. Michener, 1844; and James P. Hutcherson.

Nearly all Friends Meetings had schools connected with them, prior to the founding of the public-school system. As early as 1793, there was a school at the Gwynedd Friends Meetinghouse. It was one of the four schools in Gwynedd Township following the adoption of the public-school system in 1840 and it was supported partly by the meeting and partly by the township. The male teacher employed there was paid twenty dollars a month. Possibly, the younger women whose names are on the quilt attended the Gwynedd Friends Meeting School with Mary and Lydia.

This magnificent quilt has a history of use by the Walton family. A light background chintz separates the rows of diagonally set Album blocks. A chintz with a darker background borders the quilt. The setting triangles in the center of the quilt are dark green print, while those near the quilt's border are a lighter print.

Both chintz patterns may have come from the same piece of cloth. It was not unusual for chintz to be printed in bands of floral stripes. A wise quiltmaker could cut the fabric apart and have two patterns to work with in her design.

11. *Variable Star Strippy, c. 1840, origin unknown, 85 x 83½ inches, pieced cottons. (Collection of Sharon Yenter, In the Beginning—Quilts)*

Scraps of chintz were also used in strippy quilts, such as the one shown in no. 11. It was necessary to piece these small scraps of chintz taken from a sample book to make the strips that divide the Variable Star blocks. While some of these early strippy quilts were utilitarian projects using fabrics from the scrap basket, others were designed to showcase particular fabrics.

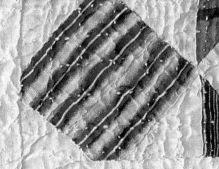

Chapter 3
A VERY SPECIAL PRESENTATION

PRESENTATION QUILTS

Presentation quilts were a popular means for expressing appreciation for a family member, special friend, or esteemed community leader such as a minister, teacher, or politician. Several varieties of presentation quilts flourished, and they differed as to the number of makers, signature of the blocks, and types of blocks used.

If the quilt were being made for a minister by the ladies of the church, it was often a group effort done over a period of time. The women seemed to work on the quilt collectively rather than as individuals, so they signed the quilt with the name of the Ladies Aid or mission society instead of placing individual signatures on the blocks. The actual quilting was also done as a group, allowing the members the opportunity to plan one of their favorite social functions, a quilting bee.

PRESIDENT'S WREATH

The President's Wreath quilt, shown in no. 15, was made as a presentation quilt for Reverend Martin J. and Elizabeth Eliza Carothers on the occasion of their marriage, 16 March 1849. Indeed, Martin was the esteemed member of the community for whom the quilt was made, for his name and the date appear quite prominently in one of the eighteen-inch diamond spaces between the blocks. Elizabeth's name is quilted upside down in a much smaller area, two by six inches, near the top border.

Martin, born in 1825, was the son of William M. and Fanny Clark Carothers of West Pennsborough Township, Pennsylvania. He was the minister for the Evangelical Association in Mt. Rock., Pennsylvania. Mt. Rock was the center of activity in Pennsborough Township, Cumberland County, when the Chambers-

Inscription block: Martin J. Carothers, March 16, 1849

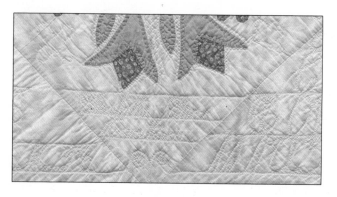

Inscription: Elizabeth Eliza Carothers

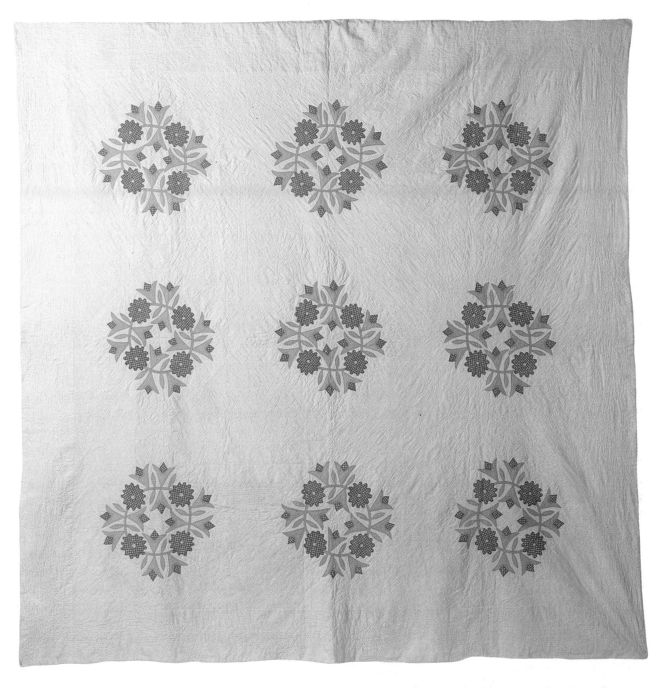

*15. President's Wreath, 1846,
Cumberland County, Pennsylvania,
95 x 95 inches, appliquéd cottons.
(Collection of Nancy J. Martin)*

burg Turnpike was built. In addition to a store and a tavern, it had a wagonmaker's and a blacksmith's shop. There was also a tailor, shoemaker, cooper, brick-maker, and butcher, as well as a distillery. The township elections and the musterings and review of the old militia were also held there.

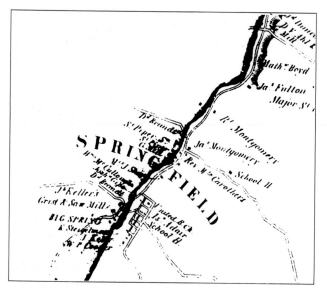

*Plot map of Springfield,
Cumberland County, Pa., 1858*

*Inscription: 1849, March 21,
Cumberland County. The rose is
red, the rest is green.*

All religious denominations met for worship in the schoolhouse until about 1846, when the Disciples, sometimes called the Campbellites, gained strength in the area. A great deal of controversy arose, and the members of the Evangelical Association united with others to build a church in which all but the Disciples would be welcomed. The church was accordingly built, and the original terms are still in adherence.

*Community Church,
Mount Rock, Pa.*

As the local minister, Martin was often called upon to witness wills and other important documents or serve as the executor of an estate. Martin was able to read and write, while some of his more wealthy landowning neighbors were not.

For his marriage to Elizabeth, the ladies of the church decided to make a quilt. They presented the quilt top to Martin and Elizabeth on their wedding day, 16 March 1849. The quilt was signed with the initials "L.W. M. Pa," possibly indicating the Ladies Work Mission of Pennsylvania. They also quilted this legend into the quilt: "1849, March 21, Cumberland County, the rose is red, the rest is green." March 21 was probably the day they completed the quilting, and knowing fabrics could fade, the ladies wanted to indicate the original color of their work. They must have been very proud of their handiwork, since it is unusual for a quilt to be so well documented.

The quilt consists of nine appliqué blocks done in the President's Wreath pattern. These eighteen-inch blocks are set together diagonally, leaving four large open spaces for quilting. The quilting stitches indicate that a number of different people worked on the quilt, covering it both with elaborate and primitive quilting designs. There is a tree (Tree of Life?), oak leaves, and a hand. There are scissors quilted in several places on the quilt. One wonders if they just traced around the items lying on the quilt, such as the hand and scissors, and then quilted, or if the scissors indicated their feelings toward Elizabeth. It was considered bad luck according to local folklore to give scissors or knives as a wedding gift. Both the scissors motif and the small space used to stitch her name may indicate that the ladies of the church were less than pleased with Martin's marriage to Elizabeth.

A crude feather design is stitched in the border. The backing is a coarse muslin, which was turned to the front as an edge finish.

SIGNATURE QUILTS

I have documented three signature quilts made in Chester County, Pennsylvania, between 1845 and 1849 (nos. 16, 17, and 18). Two of these signature quilts came from Quaker families (members of the Religious Society of Friends). The Quakers, well known for their meticulous record keeping, were quite prominent in Chester County, and their meetinghouses are excellent historical resources.

All three of these Chester County signature quilts were done in a red-and-green color combination, a popular color scheme from about 1840 until the end of the century.

Signature quilts (quilts composed of signed blocks) were a popular type of presentation quilt. They were of two types: friendship quilts, where each signed block is made from the same pattern (see no. 18) and album quilts, which are assembled with signed blocks made from different appliquéd or pieced patterns.

Signature quilts were enormously popular across the United States from 1840 to 1860. Jessica Nicoll studied forty examples made in the Middle Atlantic states between 1841 and 1855:

"Signature quilts were commemorative artifacts. Many were made by individuals, either for themselves or as a gift for a particularly dear family member or friend. Many others were made collaboratively by a group of people for presentation to a member of their community. These quilts were frequently made in acknowledgment of special occasions, such as births, marriages, and retirements, but just as often the only

Quilting at the Westown Friends School. (Photo courtesy of Chester County Historical Society)

16. James Family Album Quilt, 1845, Chester County, Pennsylvania, 72½ x 84 inches, appliquéd cottons. (Private collection)

They had three children: Ann, Charles, and William.

Martha Ann had much time for needlework and dressmaking, since Abraham's work took him across the country and back. Her exquisite appliqué album quilt, shown in no. 16, contains many excellent samples of scherenschnitte-type blocks. The quilt contains thirty-eight blocks, appliquéd in tiny stitches, indicating the blocks were made by only one person, most probably Martha Ann. Most of the blocks have signatures, either stamped or handwritten. Perhaps this top was a presentation quilt for Martha Ann and Abraham before one of their frequent moves. They moved from West Chester to Chicago, when Abraham accepted a position with the Illinois Central Railroad. Due to

failing health, he resigned and joined an older brother, who had gone to California in 1849 and was now engaged in mining operations.

When Abraham returned to Chicago, he became aware of an unusual psychic power he possessed. He was said to have used this power to locate the first artesian well in Chicago.

Abraham became involved in a series of ventures, including oil production, and made thousands of dollars. His gift as a medium secured him many lucrative positions. Several articles have been published in religious and philosophical journals documenting Abraham's "mediumship" or spiritualism.

Martha Ann and Abraham moved to Fredonia,

17. *Oxford Female Seminary Album Quilt, 1846, Chester County, Pennsylvania, 100 x 100 inches, appliquéd and pieced cottons. (Collection of Chester County Historical Society)*

New York, in 1870. Martha Ann died 10 January 1902, and their daughter Anna, who never married, attended to Abraham, until he died 7 November 1906.

The Oxford Female Seminary quilt, shown in no. 17, was made by the students and teachers for their departing principal and teacher, Reverend James Grier Ralston, in 1846.

Oxford was a small farming community in southwestern Chester County, Pennsylvania. Its population in 1837 was between fifty to one hundred people,

depending on whether you counted only the people who lived inside the borough limits (Oxford was incorporated in 1833) or also included those on the surrounding farms. Oxford was a crossroads for travelers on the Baltimore and Philadelphia Pike, as well as the Lancaster-Wilmington Road. It was centrally placed between these main centers of commerce, having no industry of its own other than a brickyard. Travelers could refresh themselves at one of the two small taverns or see to their horses' comfort or wagon repair at the blacksmith's. There were also two general

Oxford, Pennsylvania, c. 1845.
Oxford Female Seminary was
located in building on far left.
(Photo courtesy of Judith Slicer)

stores and a tailor's shop.

"The Oxford Female Seminary was founded in 1837 for the purpose of training young women for the teaching profession. An 1841 school brochure listed required courses, among them reading, plain and ornamental penmanship, English grammar, composition, general history, algebra, botany, Biblical, Grecian, and Roman antiquities, intellectual and moral philosophy, rhetoric, and logic."[22]

Besides moral science, the Bible, and teaching skills, the girls were also taught proper etiquette, how to attract a young man's attention in a ladylike manner, how to get on and off a horse properly, and how to be proper ladies in both fashion and manner-

isms. The school was founded by an ordained Presbyterian minister, John Miller Dickey, whose family came to this country from Northern Ireland in 1730. Reverend Dickey was a forward-thinking man, who not only started this seminary for young women but also founded, in 1854, Lincoln University, the first chartered school to grant academic degrees to Negro youth.

Reverend Dickey was one of ten community leaders who served as trustees when the Oxford Female Seminary received its charter in 1839. Reverend James Grier Ralston was hired as teacher and principal in 1841. Reverend Dickey and his two brothers also taught at the school. The brothers were Samuel, also a Presbyterian minister, and Ebinezer, a physician.

Early newspaper ads (1839, 1840) show the school eventually grew to become a boarding school. It was comprised of a series of buildings, housing almost one hundred students. While Reverend Ralston was there, many of the students were day students who lived in Oxford or the surrounding areas of Jennersville and East Nottingham Township. However, young ladies living in Lancaster County or those from Maryland had to board, since roads were quite poor in those days, and daily travel on these roads would have been too time-consuming.

Reverend Ralston left the school in 1845 to start a school of his own, Oakland Female Institute, in Norristown. Upon his departure, a quilt was made as a farewell present from the students and teachers.

Reverend Ralston's sister Mary A. Ralston of Hopewell, New Jersey, could have been the organizer of the quilt, since she made two blocks and dated them. His sister Frances G. Dickey, the wife of teacher Ebinezer Dickey, and Reverend Ralston's wife, Mary, who was a teacher at the seminary, also each made a block.

Red and green was probably the intended color scheme, since all the blocks, except the one in the lower left corner, were done in red-and-green cotton prints. This deviant block is an Oak Leaf pattern made from a blue-green and brown print. Several blocks are duplicates, suggesting a lack of a specific plan or directions for the makers of the blocks.

The quilting patterns are all geometric grids and vary from one block to the next; however, the quilting is nicely executed. The quilt front is folded over to the back as an edge finish.

The friendship quilt shown in no. 18 contains an inscription block that has been recorded in ink. It reads "Jane S. Webb, East Marlborough, Chester County, 1847."

All forty-nine blocks in the quilt, which was pieced from an unknown pattern, were signed in ink. The handwriting is different for each block, and several blocks are stamped, suggesting that the people signed their own blocks. Both men's and women's signatures appear on the quilt, and several blocks include the names of nearby towns such as London Grove or Unionville.

Although the quilt has descended through the family of James and Sarah Cloud, whose married names are on one of the blocks, the quilt was made for Sarah's sister, Jane S. Webb. Jane was one of ten

Inscription block

children born to Thomas and Esther Paxson Webb. Thomas Webb was a farmer and miller who lived in Kennett Township, Chester County, Pennsylvania. Jane married William Taylor, who was also a farmer. The Taylors are recorded as living in East Marlboro Township by the 1850 census. Jane died on 10 July 1887, and the unassembled friendship blocks were passed on to her sister Sarah.

Friends Meeting House, Kennett Square, Pa. (Photo courtesy of Chester County Historical Society)

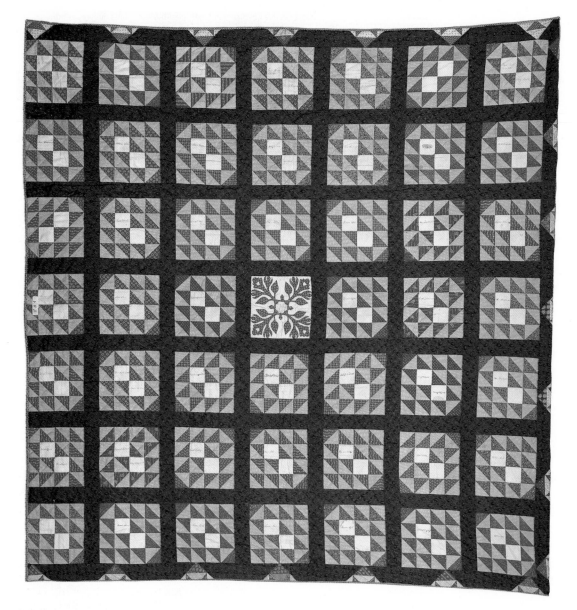

18. Webb Friendship Quilt, 1849,
Chester County, Pennsylvania,
89 x 92½ inches, appliquéd
cottons. (Private collection)

Sarah Webb was born 26 February 1817. She married James Cloud, Jr., who was born 22 July 1817. The births of their four children were recorded in the family Bible: William J., Edward P., Thomas Allen, and Mary Belle.

Mary Belle, both a stitcher and quilter, was married to a cousin, James P. Cloud, on 5 March 1885. She was close to her brother Thomas, a physician, who never married.

When Thomas died in 1896, Mary Belle and her mother, Sarah, assembled and quilted the friendship blocks made for Jane in 1847. Sarah and Mary Belle included a tribute to Thomas on the quilt and quilted the initials "TAC" and "1898" into the quilt. Sarah died in 1899, at the age of 82. The quilt now belongs to Mary Belle's grandson, Joseph Hannum.

Many members of the Webb and Cloud families are buried in the churchyard of the Old Kennett Meetinghouse. We know that quilting bees were common in the Kennett Square area, through references in historical novels: "Aunt Eliza has an old woman's quilting-party, and they'll stay all night. . . ."[23]

*19. Freedom Quilt, c. 1850,
Sharpsburg, Virginia, 83 x 93 inches,
pieced cottons. (Private collection)*

FREEDOM QUILTS

Another type of presentation quilt was the freedom quilt, which was presented to a young man when he became twenty-one to signify his independence. Stories of freedom quilts abound in quilting mythology, yet few freedom quilts have been documented.

According to Ruth Finley, "In the old days a youth's arrival at years of legal discretion was an important event. No longer could his parents or guardian bind him out as an apprentice, take his wages, make him work at home for nothing or legally restrain his actions in any way. He was free. Wealthy parents, copying the time-honored custom of England as observed especially in the case of an eldest son, made of a boy's twenty-first birthday an affair of great display. In families of more modest income an evening 'company' was the order of the day, in honor of which occasion the young man wore his 'freedom suit.' Even bound boys were given a new suit of clothes by the master from

whose service their twenty-first birthday released them.

"The 'Freedom Quilt' was the gift of a lad's feminine friends. His mother or sisters invited the girls of his acquaintance to spend the afternoon preceding the supper. They came, bringing with them scraps of their prettiest gowns, and from these they pieced the young man's quilt, in reality for his future wife. For a boy's 'Freedom Quilt' was always laid carefully away against the time when he might add it as his gift to the dowry chest of his bride-to-be."[24]

The freedom quilt, shown in no. 19, was purchased by a quilt collector from an antique dealer in Virginia. The following note was attached: "Made by Ida Reynolds, 1851, Sharpsburg, Virginia." After returning home, she noticed the "21" stenciled near the border. The fabrics, especially the chintz border, support the 1851 date of the quilt, but it is difficult to establish Ida Reynolds and Sharpsburg, especially since Sharpsburg, Virginia, does not exist today.

Chapter 4

APPLIQUÉ QUILTS

BEST QUILTS

The appliqué quilt traditionally has been made as a "best" quilt because of the time and effort involved. These quilts were usually made of the finest fabrics and covered with lavish quilting, executed in the most delicate stitches. Most quilters left ample "white space" or open space between their appliqué designs to show off their quilting. Often, swirling appliqué borders would surround the quilt. Because these were saved as best quilts, many have survived to this day in fairly good condition.

While much of women's domestic sewing was for practical purposes, women also needed to make best quilts as gifts, or for weddings, births, or other special occasions. Patricia Mainardi speculates as to why women enjoyed making them:

"These (appliqué) are the ones that women considered their 'best' quilts, and which, although fewer of them were made, have survived in larger number because of their 'show,' rather than 'everyday' use. Because of the greater freedom of the appliqué technique, women created hundreds of new designs, most based on natural forms, especially the flowers they loved." [25]

These best quilts were rarely, if ever, used. When they were put on the bed for guests or special occasions, the curtains would be drawn to prevent fading. Special cases, much like a pillowcase, were sometimes made from the same fabric as the quilt and used to protect the quilt in storage. Appliqué quilts were given such special care that many have been found in fresh, never-washed condition, with the penciled quilting design still visible.

PENNSYLVANIA DUTCH TULIP APPLIQUÉ

The floral appliqué quilt shown in no. 20 was probably made by Christina Wolfgang in 1859. The fact that this was a special quilt is signified by the date that was quilted twice along the border. One of these dates has been quilted over in dark thread. Also quilted between the stem and leaf motifs in the border is the word "Citregt B. N. A." or "Citrest B. N. A." The significance of these letters is not known.

Christina was from a Lutheran family who lived in Earl Township, Berks County, Pennsylvania. The quilt was made five years before her marriage to William Clauser, 19 March 1864. The Pennsylvania Dutch (Pennsylvania Deutsch or German) influence is evident in this design, with its large-scale tulips in red fabric that has faded to tannish brown. The stylized stem-and-leaf arrangement fills the block. These twenty-

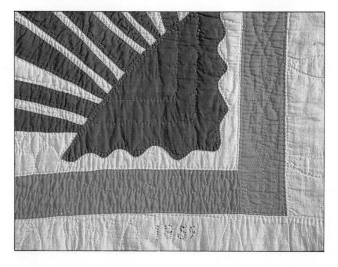

1859 date

20. Tulip, 1859, Berks County, Pennsylvania, 82 x 82 inches, appliquéd cottons. (Collection of Ann Stohl)

six-inch blocks are bordered by a narrow, bright strip of fabric and a wide border featuring a stem-and-leaf quilting design. The homespun muslin backing has a separate fabric binding. Pennsylvania Dutch quilts have always been readily identifiable, as Ruth E. Finley relates in her book, published in 1929: "Pennsylvania Dutch quilts are easiest of all to identify. They are usually gaudier in color, bolder and more elaborate in design, pieced oftener than appliquéd and superlative in quilting."[26]

Mrs. Finley also speculates on why these women made such elaborate quilts: "Book-learning was despised—certainly for women. Anything but manual labor and its material results was a waste of time. Few Pennsylvania Dutch girls in early days were even taught to read. As for the boys, enough 'larnin' to keep them from being cheated in a trade was not out of place, 'figgerin' being considered by far the most important of the three R's. Perhaps no family life anywhere in this country, at any time, was so restricted as that of the unadulterated Pennsylvania Dutch farmer, the narrowness of whose thrift has become proverbial. And it may have been some unconsciously craved compensation for the drab monotony of their days that caused the women of these households to evolve quilt patterns so intricate."[27]

*21. Feather Appliqué, c. 1880,
Georgia, 81 x 81 inches, appliquéd
cottons. (Collection of Nancy J.
Martin)*

FEATHER APPLIQUÉ

The Feather Appliqué (c. 1840) shown in no. 21 was made by Ora Lee Watson. Ora Lee was originally from a farm near Aiken, South Carolina. She married a man who was also named Watson, and they moved to Augusta, South Carolina. Ora had a daughter, who, in 1901, died in childbirth, leaving three children. Ora raised the youngest of these, Ava Carlisle, until she was ten years old. Ava was separated from her brother and sister, who were raised by their father. Ora must have had a special fondness for Ava, because the quilt was left to her.

This pattern could be based on either a feather or a tobacco leaf. Averil Colby cites its popularity and speculates as to its source: "The feather pattern is one which undoubtedly originated as a quilting pattern. It is common and popular in English and American work,

whether in applied work or quilting. . . . It has been suggested that Princess Feather, which is an American name and not used in England, may have been inspired by the feathered headdress of an Indian princess."[28] But, the pattern does bear an amazing similarity to the Tobacco Leaf pattern, which originated in Virginia.

The nine 25-inch blocks are made from bright gold-and-green print fabrics and bordered by a solid red swag. The gold portion of the feathers is done in reverse appliqué. The quilt is heavily quilted both on top of the appliqué and in the white space. One would think that this quilt was made for show, but according to a friend of Ava's (Ava died in 1986), this quilt was used by both the Watson and Carlisle families. There is a red border, which was cut down when the original binding was replaced. A rainbow or Baptist Fan pattern is quilted in the border. The backing fabric is the same quality as that used for the appliqué block on the quilt front.

22. Oak Leaf and Reel, c. 1885, origin unknown, 87 x 87 inches, appliquéd cottons. (Collection of Sharon Yenter, In the Beginning—Quilts)

OAK LEAF AND REEL

There are many variations of Oak Leaf patterns or the Charter Oak. The quilt shown in no. 22 is an interesting version with a pieced center. The twenty-five red-yellow-and-green blocks are set "on point," leaving large, open spaces for quilting. The quilt is exquisitely quilted with a one-inch grid. Green piping has been added around the border and at the outside edges.

The Oak Leaf and Reel is a very old pattern and has been found in album quilts dated 1818, 1830, and 1839. The Oak Leaf pattern was often found in friendship quilts, since the oak represented steadfastness. The Reel design, which often incorporated leaves, predates the album quilts of the 1840s. Variations of the Reel design are found in quilts dating as early as 1818.[29]

23. Pomegranate, 1880,
Glenconda, Illinois, 92½ x 94
inches, appliquéd cottons.
(Collection of Nancy J. Martin)

POMEGRANATE QUILT

The Pomegranate quilt (no. 23) was made in 1880 by Janie Jackson Orr of Hardin County, Illinois. The Orr family descended from Irish immigrants, who first stopped off in Ohio. Early census records of Hardin County show a Samuel Orr, born in Ireland, living in Hardin County. According to family tradition, one of the Orrs, born in Ireland, received land in what is now Hardin County as payment for service in the army during the War of 1812 with England. The Orrs added to that land by homesteading and purchasing land until they had roughly three hundred acres.

Joseph Bonaparte Orr was born in Galliopolis, Ohio. He came to Hardin County as a young man and settled on the land. He married a neighbor, Sara Williams, a member of another one of the early families settling in the county. Joseph and Sarah had six children: William, James, Joseph, Nancy J., David, and Mary Elizabeth. William died in infancy; James died as a result of illness at the end of the Civil War, in which he served; Joseph died accidentally or was murdered (the family never knew for sure), when he was returning home in 1873 from the gold rush in California; Nancy J. died in 1858; Mary Elizabeth never married. She helped take care of her mother and lived until 1913. Joseph Bonaparte Orr died young and left David at the age of twelve to help his mother run the farm. David eventually took control of the three-hundred-acre homeplace.

On 16 October 1890, David married Jane Jackson, daughter of James Monroe Jackson, and moved to the river farm on the Jackson place, keeping the original Orr farm. The river farm contained 550 acres. (James M. Jackson was the first native-born Hardin Countian, according to family tradition.) The Orrs welcomed the marriage, since the Jacksons were "up-to-date people" and among the "most respected people."

Janie Jackson Orr is described by her daughter-in-law, Roxanne Orr, as a "wonderful Christian woman." Born in 1873, Janie lived in Hardin County all of her life, "right below Elizabethtown." She gave birth to her first son, Clausie, in 1892 and David in 1894 but died in childbirth in 1896. Roxanna also noted that "she was getting up there when she married."

Janie was an expert needlewoman who created many fine quilts. Janie's mother and sister made quilts, and all three of them sometimes worked together on the quilting. Janie even made her own thread for the quilts. She also made her own clothing and enjoyed doing cross-stitch and needlepoint. David Orr, Jr., (Janie's son) married Roxanna Tyler in 1917. Roxanna inherited Janie's Pomegranate quilt and her cross-stitch but never got to meet the wonderful woman who made them.

The Pomegranate blocks in Janie's quilt are small in size (thirteen inches) for appliqué blocks. Solid-color fabrics in red, gold, and two shades of a home-dyed green were placed on a white background. One surmises that, since the green for the blocks on the left side and the green for the border are different, the maker ran out of green fabric and had to dye more. Either the quality of the fabric or a change in the dye recipe accounts for the change in color.

The Pomegranate blocks are joined with six-inch-wide strips of white lattice, showing that the maker intended to showcase her quilting and not the blocks. In fact, most Pomegranate quilts have the blocks set in groups of four or in a more interesting arrangement. A rainbow or Baptist Fan pattern is beautifully quilted across the quilt's surface, continuing through the appliqué. The borders were appliquéd before they were joined to the quilt top, so the design does not continue around the corners. The backing appears to be a coarse homespun fabric. The original green binding has been replaced.

The Pomegranate, or Love Apple pattern, was a popular one during the 1840s through 1860s, and the origin of the name is unclear. A Mountain Mist pattern, published in the early 1900s, relates the Love Apple pattern to the pomegranate. Ruth Finley, however, relates the Love Apple pattern to the tomato plant:

"This quilt undoubtedly was known by other names, but the oldest and most interesting was that once given the now widely used vegetable—the tomato.

"It was not until about the middle of the nineteenth century that this ordinary food was considered edible. A native of the tropics, it probably was introduced into New England by seafaring men engaged in West India trade. Sailors brought all sorts of things home to their families—parrots, cloisonne, Oriental silks and embroideries, monkeys, carved ivory chessmen . . . and walrus teeth. The tomato plant with its bright red fruit appealed to the garden-loving women. Known as 'Love Apple,' it was much admired, often grown, but never eaten."[30]

Jane Nelson Fleming

Ada Belle Whitney

TULIP QUILT

The lovely red Tulip quilt (no. 24) was appliquéd in 1852 by Jane Nelson Fleming in Ithaca, New York, at the Nelson family farm. Jane was born on 17 May 1836, the oldest child of Eleanor and Phineas Nelson. The quilt was pieced before Jane met and married James Stringer Fleming on 23 March 1858. James and Jane had five children within a ten-year span. The oldest of these was Ada Belle Fleming, born on 22 February 1859.

Jane later quilted the top and gave it to her daughter Ada Belle for her wedding in 1882. Two of these dates are quilted into the quilt as inscriptions. Ada Belle was eighteen when she married Frank Witney. She was proud of Frank, who was a man of many talents: a minister of the Baptist church and a newspaper editor and publisher. Ada Belle was said to be very attractive.

Shortly after her marriage, there was an epidemic (the family seems to think it was yellow fever) and all of the Nelsons except Ada Belle fell ill. She nursed her parents and brothers and sisters, who were ill with chills and fever. Only her brother Thomas recovered; her mother and sister died in 1883, her brother in 1884, and her father in 1885. This happened during the period when she gave birth to her first two children.

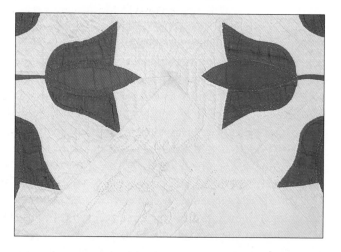

Inscription block

Inscription block

24. Tulip, 1856, New York,
72 x 80 inches, appliquéd cottons.
(Private collection)

Ada Belle and Frank moved to Rochester, Minnesota, where Frank continued his ministry. They had seven children, the youngest of which was Albert, who dearly loved his mother and passed on his treasured memories to his daughter, Adabelle. They were not a wealthy family, but placed a high value on education. The entire family, along with several members of Frank's congregation, moved to Yakima, Washington, in 1907 and purchased rights in a peach orchard enterprise. The enterprise failed and Frank turned to other means, in addition to his ministry, to support the family. He purchased a newspaper, the *Yakima Independent,* which family members, including his son Albert, helped him run. Albert married Elinor Greenleaf. They published a newspaper in Oak Harbor, Washington, and then moved to Bellevue to purchase the *Bellevue American* newspaper. Albert's daughter

Adabelle (named for her grandmother) inherited the treasured quilt.

Each appliqué Tulip block in the quilt measures thirteen by thirteen inches. The red-and-green tulips are grouped in sets of four. The twelve blocks are then set on the diagonal, with a hanging-diamonds pattern quilted in these blocks. The quilting in the tulip blocks outlines each shape, and a straight-line grid fills the remainder of the space. A nine-inch-wide, striped border frames the quilt on three sides and has a checkerboard pattern in the lower corners.

There is a lightweight batting in the quilt, and the fine muslin backing has been turned to the front of the quilt as an edge finish. It was stitched by a machine that produced a straight stitch on the quilt's front and a chain stitch on the backing.

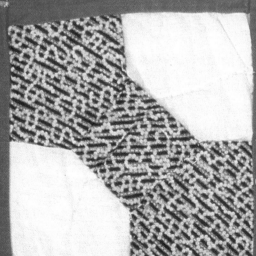

Chapter 5

PATCHWORK
PLEASURES

THE PLEASURES OF PIECING

While appliqué quilts were made as "best" quilts, pieced or patchwork quilts were usually less magnificent. Intended for everyday use and often made from scraps rather than newly purchased fabric, many of these patchwork quilts have an amazing number of pieces. No scrap of fabric was considered too small or unsuitable for the scrap bag; any piece could be used for a patchwork quilt. Depending on the quiltmaker's artistic ability and sense of color, many quilts that capture both our eyes and heart were created from the scrap bag.

The majority of America's patchwork quilts were stitched between 1840 and 1870, often by women who were part of our country's westward migration or who lived far away from fabric suppliers. Scrap bags were filled with the good material left in cast-off clothing, tired household linens, and leftover scraps of fresh material used to make the family's clothing. A study of the fabric in many patchwork quilts will reveal such diverse fabrics as shirtings used to produce garments for the men of the family; homespun used for towels, linens, and aprons; dark prints used for women's blouses (waists, as they were called in the 1870s); and even fancier dress goods in families fortunate enough to have special clothes for "Sunday best."

In the early part of the nineteenth century, women spent part of each day producing their own cloth. This industry included producing raw material, either wool or flax on the farm, through the various stages to clothing or bedding. It wasn't until midcentury that factories replaced the home in the work of textile manufacturing.[31]

By the midnineteenth century, quiltmakers who had the means could purchase American fabrics for their quilts. America's cotton-printing industry began to compete with the European printers in price, quality, and selection. Changes in dye technology produced bright, fast colors such as chrome orange, chrome yellow, double pink (a speckled pink created by printing a dark shade of pink over a light shade of pink), and purple. "Purple was such a popular color that it was classified as a 'staple' by fabric manufacturers. Some women bought purples because they believed it would last longer than the brighter, more colorful prints."[32]

By midcentury there was also an assortment of patterns and designs that women had knowledge of and used in their quilts. These patterns were traded and circulated informally among quilters, for printed publication of quilt patterns did not take place until later in the nineteenth century.

From existing artifacts, we can speculate as to the means by which quilt patterns circulated. Patterns for patchwork and quilting from cut tin were produced by tinsmiths. These patterns were sold by both itinerant peddlers and tinsmiths who traveled from town to town. Florence Peto, noted quilt historian, feels these patterns were part of their stock in trade: "In Johanna Bergen's Diary, kept on a Flatlands, Long Island farm between 1824–1829, she says: 'Peddler here today, took dinner with us, we made no trade with him.' In the 1840's, in Pennsylvania, a peddler stayed overnight with one family; when the womenfolk deplored the fact they had no new quilt patterns with which to work, he asked for paper and scissors and proceeded to cut a design which, unfolded, revealed scrolls, leaves and complicated curlicues resembling those on old lacy valentines. From the pattern a quilt was made in dull yellow calico appliquéd to a brown cambric background—it may be seen in the collection at Landis Valley Museum, Lancaster, Pennsylvania."[33]

Often, quilters made sample blocks to record quilt patterns. They kept these blocks as a record or exchanged them with other quilters. Several authors have commented on the existence of these blocks:

"Many of the quilt blocks we find today were sample pattern blocks never meant to be incorporated into a quilt top. . . ."[34]

"It was customary to make a block of a pattern to keep for reference, and some quilters had a collection of blocks, occasionally with the name of the pattern pinned to the block."[35]

"A new design would be held in memory and the block pieced when the seamstress was back in her house to be stored as a 'sketch' for further reproduction. . . ."[36]

The existence of these block collections was studied by Wilene Smith, who has purchased eight of these collections. "Some were large collections containing more than 75 examples while others were small in scope. In each case the fabrics in the blocks generally span a century in time (as early as the 1840s continuing into the 1930s) and, overall, each block was of a different design. Many of them were badly stained, their fabrics softened by much handling down through the years."[37]

Regional quilt studies and registrations have documented additional block collections in Canada, Pennsylvania, and throughout the South.

Publication of patterns was found infrequently in the midnineteenth century, with an occasional pattern found in *Godey's Lady's Book and Magazine* or other needlework books. Even magazines geared for the rural reader, such as *Farm and Fireside* and *Farmer's Wife,* did not print quilt patterns until the 1900s.

Mail-order companies, which were appealing and convenient for rural readers, were established as early as 1872 (Montgomery Ward). Sears, Roebuck's 1891 catalog featured an eight-page insert on jewelry and sewing machines. The size of both companies' catalogs quickly increased, making it necessary to divide the catalogs into departments. Both Sears, Roebuck & Co. and Montgomery Ward featured dry-goods departments, which carried domestics, fabrics, batting, and patterns. The 1900 edition of the Sears catalog (opening page shown below) devoted twenty pages to the dry-goods department.

Smaller specialty mail-order companies developed, such as the Ladies Art Company. Owned and managed

Opening pages of Dry Goods Department in 1900 Sears, Roebuck & Co. catalog.

Ladies Art Company catalog

by H. M. Brockstedt, this company was a mail-order source for quilt patterns, art-needlework patterns, kits, and tools. It was a family-owned-and-operated company, which began in 1875 at 209 Pine Street in St. Louis. The Ladies Art Company catalog was titled, *Diagrams of Quilt Sofa and Pin Cushion Patterns.* The eighth revised edition was printed in 1898 and contained pattern numbers 1–420. It printed small black-and-white diagrams (less than one-inch square) for each pattern offered. The patterns were packaged in a gray, waxed envelope, which was numbered. Each pattern also included the necessary templates and directions, along with a colored rendition of the quilt pattern, approximately 3½ inches square. These color cards, consisting of line drawings printed on heavy cardboard, were painted by hand.[38]

This delightful job was the after-school chore of the owner's children. The children used watercolors to paint the color cards.[39]

The color cards must have been quite popular, for some quilters collected them individually without the patterns (perhaps a forerunner of baseball cards?). The color cards sold for 4 cents each or 25 for 75 cents. Patterns that included the color cards sold for 10 cents each, 3 for 25 cents, 7 for 50 cents or 15 for $1.

The patterns shown in the Ladies Art Company catalog were both original designs and reprints of existing patterns. The catalog was revised several times, with new patterns substituted for previous patterns. Mr. Brockstedt died during the 1920s, but his family continued the business until 1940.

Templates and envelopes from the Ladies Art Company

Color cards from the Ladies Art Company

25. Four-Patch Diamond, c. 1865, Berks County, Pennsylvania, 76 x 82 inches, pieced cottons. (Collection of Ann Stohl)

FOUR-PATCH DIAMOND

This typically bright, Berks County, Pennsylvania, scrap quilt contains Four-Patch blocks, which are alternately set into a chrome yellow or double pink print background. The Four Patches were made from a random assortment of plaids, shirtings, and dress goods, suggesting they most likely came from the scrap basket. The chrome yellow and double pink prints used for the background were probably newly purchased fabric, as was the purple used for the border. The quilt's backing is a brown-checked fabric, and the binding is a separate black-and-white "mourning print."

Made by Christina Wolfgang Clauser in 1865, the quilt shown in no. 25 is typical of many utility quilts made in the Clauser family. Although made from scraps, Christina's artistic eye skillfully combined bright new fabric in an overall repetition to enliven the dark scraps. The wide purple border calms the liveliness found in the center of the quilt and enlarges the quilt to bed size.

26. Sampler, c. 1890, origin
unknown, 72 x 72 inches, pieced
cottons. (Private collection)

SAMPLER QUILT

The sampler quilt of unknown origin, shown in no. 26, was purchased as a top. The assorted sizes used for each block suggest that the blocks may have once been part of a pattern collection. Each block has been carefully hand pieced. The blocks are joined together by machine with random sashing cut from fabrics of a later vintage. The style of the quilt suggests that a utility quilt was being quickly constructed. One wonders if the original maker of the blocks had to raid her pattern collection one fall in order to construct another quilt "before the cold set in." Or was a quilt needed for

"JAY" (see block at lower right) in a short amount of time, thus necessitating an invasion of the pattern collection? Or perhaps this collection of pattern blocks came into the possession of a quilter with a "finishing compulsion," and she couldn't resist stitching the blocks into a quilt top.

The blocks themselves are a wonderful reference to the patterns available in the late 1800s, and include some original designs and variations. From the top row, left to right, are: Envelope, Cactus Basket, Bow Tie, Devil's Claw, Drunkard's Path, Sister's Choice, Broken Dishes (variation), Rolling Star, and Evening Star.

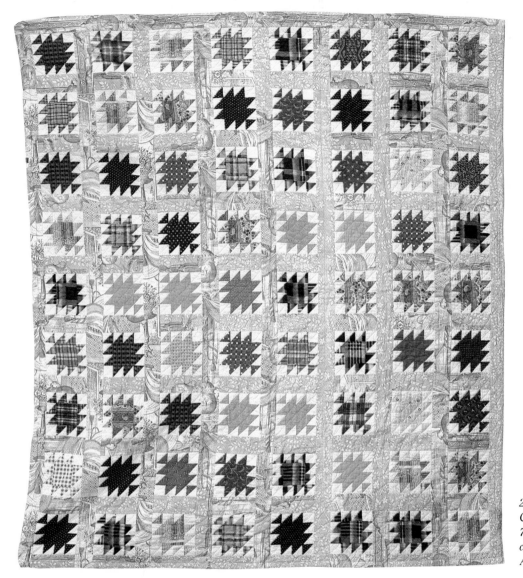

27. Anvil, c. 1870, Berks County, Pennsylvania, 75 x 80 inches, pieced cottons. (Collection of Ann Stohl)

ANVIL

The scrap quilt shown in no. 27 was made by the women of the Wolfgang-Clauser family in Berks County, Pennsylvania. These same women also made the quilts shown in nos. 8 and 25. Each Anvil or Sawtooth block is pieced from a single print fabric and muslin. Plaids, shirtings, and dress goods from the scrap basket were used to create vivid and lively blocks. The quilt is effectively joined together with a most unusual sashing fabric—a decorator print that more commonly would be used for draperies or upholstery. This fabric is of good quality and appears to have been printed with copper plates. The print is larger in scale and resembles the chintz botanical and pillar prints popular during the early nineteenth century in both England and America. It adds a light and interesting touch to what could have been a mundane scrap quilt. There is no binding on this quilt; both front and back edges have been turned to the inside as an edge finish.

Snaps still remain on the quilt's front and back for the attachment of the "whisker cloth." This cloth was a piece of fabric sewn, snapped, or buttoned to the top of the quilt, to prevent the quilt from being snagged or worn by a gentleman's rough whiskers. "Whisker cloths" were generally used on "best" quilts, which were meant to be preserved.

28. Feathered World without End, c. 1865, origin unknown, 64 x 71 inches, pieced cottons. (Collection of Jean Christensen)

FEATHERED WORLD WITHOUT END

The Feathered World without End pattern shown in no. 28 is also known as Pine Burr and Pine Cone. This interesting variation uses several different calico prints, with the red-and-blue blocks being arranged skillfully to organize the overall design. The blocks, made of blue-striped fabric, have been carefully placed to add movement to the arrangement. The blocks are set together with no sashing between. The quilt is bordered, bound, and backed with the same white fabric.

This quilt pattern is one of many with names based on Scripture. The phrase "world without end" can be found in several places in the Bible and is common to many Christian prayers: "Glory be to the Father, and to the Son, and to the Holy Ghost, as it was in the Beginning, is now and ever shall be, world without end. Amen."

America was founded on the principle of religious freedom, and many women made the church or their religion the central focus of their life. Thus, it would not be unusual to name this block, which forms a repeated pattern or overall chain, World without End. This name reflected their belief in eternal life.

29. Star within a Star, c. 1890, origin unknown, 62½ x 80 inches, pieced cottons. (Collection of Jean Christensen)

STAR WITHIN A STAR

The Star within a Star quilt shown in no. 29 is a wonderful example of a pieced scrap quilt. Various light-colored shirtings contrast with the star's center and tips, which have been pieced in shades of madder and chocolate. (Madder root was used to print fabric and produced a standard range of colors—browns, dull reds, orange, purple, and pink.) The stars are joined by green diamond-shaped pieces, then surrounded by a green border. The backing is made from woven homespun, and a separate black-and-white calico print binding has been added. A wool batting was used for filling. Each diamond shape within the star is outline quilted, with rows of straight lines in the green diamond pieces. A diagonal grid is quilted in the border.

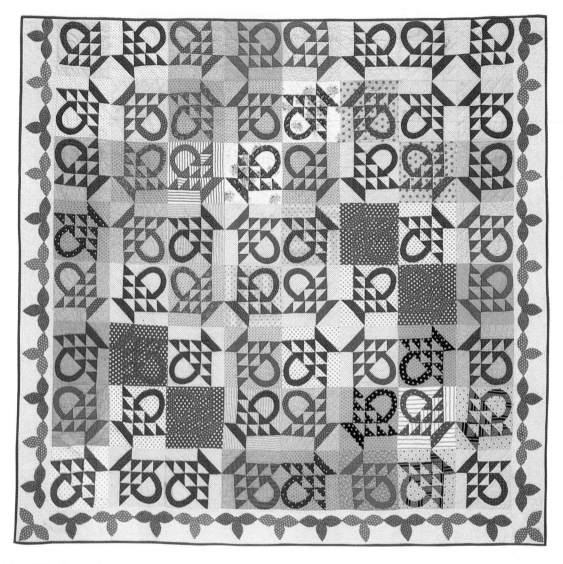

30. Basket, c. 1900, Chester County,
Pennsylvania, 83 x 90 inches, pieced
and appliquéd cottons. (Collection
of Nancy J. Martin)

BASKET

Baskets were among the most popular patterns, combining both piecing and appliqué. The earliest examples date from 1850 to 1860, and they are known by many names, such as Grandmother's Basket, Cherry Basket, Flower Basket, and Pieced Basket.

The nine-inch basket blocks made by Sara Bryans Brown and Eliza Boyd, shown in no. 30, are an exuberant display of colorful scraps. The women sat and hand pieced the blocks in the evenings at Sarah's Chester County farm, where Eliza also lived. The Basket blocks were later joined together, using the sewing machine.

The two women must have had a plan as they pieced their blocks, because the blocks were joined together in rows with the background and baskets forming diagonal patterns of color. Shirtings were the most common background fabric used in the basket blocks, but sometimes an unusual scale or color fabric, such as the bright blue polka dot, was used, enlivening the quilt. The chrome yellow prints also stand out.

An appliqué border, with pieces carefully hand stitched to shirting fabric, appears on three sides of the quilt. "Because in the evening there was little else to do, they must have made quilt top after quilt top," relates Sarah's granddaughter, Martha Kinsey.

31. Star and Crescent, c. 1880,
New Hampshire, 79 x 87 inches,
appliquéd cottons. (Collection of
Nancy J. Martin)

STAR AND CRESCENT

The Star and Crescent pattern shown in no. 31 was made by an unknown quilter in New Hampshire during the 1880s. The twenty blocks are made from red-and-white print fabrics, and each measures sixteen inches square. The diamonds in the block center are repeated in the border motif.

This quilt is entirely hand pieced, a difficult feat on the curved center pieces. Only two fabrics have been used for the center section of the quilt: a light background with a floral print set amidst a swirling beige design and a white dot fabric outlined with brown circles and printed on a red background. The brown fabric outlining the circles must have been done with a harsh aniline dye, because the fabric is deteriorating, and the circles are dropping out of the background.

Star and Crescent, which is the name Ruth Finley gave this design, is the most common name for this pattern. It also has been called Star of the West, King's Crown, Compass, the Four Winds, Star of the Four Winds, and Lucky Star and Four Winds.

GREENEVILLE STAR

Eight-pointed stars or variations of the LeMoyne Star pattern were popular all through the nineteenth century. There were many names and regional variations of this design. It was one of the earliest of all star patterns and was named after Jean Baptist LeMoyne and Pierre LeMoyne, who founded New Orleans in 1718. Through a gradual corruption of pronunciation, the LeMoyne Star became known as the Lemon Star in New England.

The variation shown in no. 32 was made by Caroline Parman Bird, the daughter of Dr. Robert Parman and Mary Anne Ruble. She was born in Greeneville, Tennessee, in September of 1882. Caroline

Caroline Parman Bird

had an older brother, Robert, who also became a doctor. After Caroline's father died, her mother married Thomas Newberry, and they had four girls.

Caroline's home life was eventful in this large family. Her brother Bob once brought friends from medical school for a visit. While they were there, they took out some of the young siblings' tonsils for practice.

Caroline married a Greeneville schoolmaster, Charles Mathias Bird. They moved to Red Rock, Oklahoma, and then Billings, Oklahoma, where their only child, Robert Parman Bird, was born in 1906. Caroline's half-sister, Mary Golda (Mamie), came to board with them. Carrie, as she was called by family, probably made her quilts while in Oklahoma. In 1921, Carrie and Charles continued their westward trek, finally settling in Seattle. They purchased an ice cream shop, calling it Bird's Queen Anne Dairy, and both worked there.

Ruth Ghromley, the daughter of Carrie's half-sister (Mamie), recalls, "Aunt Carrie Bird was old enough to be a grandmother figure to me. She sewed a great deal. She made dresses and coats for my sister and me. I was ill when I was ten and had to miss the end-of-the-year school picnic. My parents went with my sister. Aunt Carrie stayed with me and started me making a Ninepatch quilt. I made a block a day for quite a while. When I was in college, my mother had those blocks put together into a quilt for me."

Four of the star points in Carrie Parman Bird's Greeneville Star are divided into smaller diamond units. This pattern variation is unnamed, so I refer to it as Greeneville Star. Perhaps it was a regional design or had some family significance. The color scheme is also quite unusual: tobacco brown with a blue-green. It was probably made from hand-dyed fabrics that were originally red and green but faded to these colors. The large twenty-two-inch blocks are set together with a five-inch-wide lattice and smaller LeMoyne Star blocks. The backing is pieced together from coarse, irregular fabric, possibly hand woven. The quilt is magnificently quilted with a triple rainbow or fan pattern, often referred to as the Baptist Fan. It's possible this name was derived from the ladies' church groups who often marked their quilts with this pattern, tying a pencil to a string and marking arcs across the quilt. Other regional names for this quilting pattern are Shell or Elbow. The quilt is bound with a narrow binding of the blue-green fabric.

*32. Greeneville Star, c. 1900,
Oklahoma, 70 x 82 inches,
pieced cottons. (Collection of
Nancy J. Martin)*

*35. Maple Bud, c. 1900, Berks
County, Pennsylvania, 81 x 81
inches, pieced cottons. (Collection
of Nancy J. Martin)*

MAPLE BUD

The Maple Bud quilt, shown in no. 35, is probably an original design or regional variation. Purchased in Berks County, Pennsylvania, it is typical of the exuberant color schemes used in this area: chrome yellow, Turkey red, and a dark green print. The chrome yellow prints are those which were manufactured by the Ely Walker Company for over one hundred years, making it difficult to date the time the quilt was made.

The design resembles the Maple Leaf block but includes a red square in the corner of each block, possibly representing a bud. The same Turkey red fabric is used to outline each block. Four of these outlined blocks form a large block nineteen inches square. Chrome yellow sashing and a green border complete the quilt.

The blocks are machine pieced, including the stitching of the appliqué stems, where white thread was used. The backing is a light brown, figured print with the front of the quilt turned to the back as an edge finish. The Maple Bud blocks are quilted in an overall grid pattern, and an elaborate cable is stitched into the chrome yellow and green borders.

36. Hands All Around, 1895, origin unknown, 70 x 96 inches, pieced cottons. (Collection of Nancy J. Martin)

HANDS ALL AROUND

The Hands All Around quilt shown in no. 36 was made in a patriotic color scheme, most likely from a supply of scraps. Although there was enough of the same background fabric for each block and sashing square and also enough Turkey red for the sashing, scraps of fabric were used to hand piece the remainder of the block.

The background fabric features horseshoes and riding crops, two very popular motifs found in shirting prints during the 1890s. The sashing is a coarsely woven fabric in the popular Turkey red color. Indigo blue fabrics, including calicoes, chambrays, and sateen, were used for the main design of these twenty-inch blocks. Several blocks were completed in different prints when the maker ran out of her original fabric.

LILIES ALL AROUND

The original design shown in no. 37 appears to be a variation of the Hands All Around design. Augusta Melvina Ballard combined piecing with appliqué, which is used for the buds and leaves, when she made this quilt around 1900.

Augusta Melvina Rosa was born in England on 29 March 1867 and immigrated to Wisconsin with her family. Augusta married a mule trader, George A. Ballard, and they lived in Beloit, Wisconsin. She had two sons, George Lysle, Jr., and Lloyd Vernon.

Augusta was an accomplished needlewoman who did beautiful crochet work and sewing. She would make a dress for her granddaughter Virginia on every birthday. She also made Virginia's first long dress for a very special "garden party." Augusta crocheted intricate borders and edges on all of her linens. She taught her son George to knit, and it was George who taught knitting to his daughter, Virginia.

Augusta made many quilts, including this unusual variation. Each fifteen-inch block is hand pieced with precision. The petals of the lily are of a solid-color Turkey red fabric. The lily's base, the center section of the block, and the appliqué pieces use varying green print fabrics, suggesting a scrap-basket project.

The Lily blocks are set alternately with plain white blocks, but, since an even number of blocks is used in each row, the design lacks symmetry. The quilting lines were marked with a type of blue pencil that cannot be removed. It was more common to use a lead pencil for marking, since this leaves only a soft shadow that can be removed with washing. The quilting stitches are neat and even. A solid white backing has been turned to the front and used as an edge finish.

Ballard home in Beloit, Wisconsin

Augusta Melvina Ballard

*37. Lilies All Around, c. 1900,
Wisconsin, 72 x 76 inches, pieced
and appliquéd cottons. (Collection
of Nancy J. Martin)*

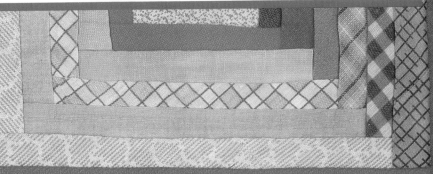

Chapter 6

SUNSHINE AND
SHADOWS

LIGHT AND DARK VARIATIONS

Log Cabin quilt patterns and their variations, such as Courthouse Steps and Pineapple, derive their names and design from the arrangement of the dark and light sides of the blocks. This type of overall light and dark pattern became so pleasing, that quilters began to set other blocks in these light and dark arrangements.

The most common Log Cabin arrangements are Sunshine and Shadows, where the four dark sides and four light sides of the block meet; Straight Furrows, where the light and dark sides form diagonal bands of color across the quilt top; Barn Raising, which has the colors alternating concentrically from the center; and Zig Zag, which forms bands of color that zigzag across the quilt.

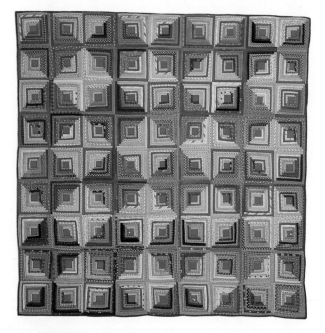

38. *Wool Log Cabin, c. 1890,*
origin unknown, 74 x 74 inches,
pieced wools. (Collection of
Nancy J. Martin)

The Log Cabin quilt pattern first appeared around 1860 and remained extremely popular until 1930. Early examples were made from silk, wool, and challis, as well as cotton. Many of them were pieced directly to a foundation block.

The Log Cabin block is full of American pioneer symbolism. It was popular for politicians to trace their roots to a log cabin, suggesting a humble beginning or "a man of the people." The strips of fabric symbolized the logs from which the cabin was built, row upon row. The Barn Raising set represented the logs and boards of a barn that neighbors gathered to help erect, and the Straight Furrows variation referred to the patterns plowed in the field. Zig Zag symbolized the stacked, split rail fences, which enclosed the pioneer family's cabin. The color used in the block was also symbolic: red in the center squares for the hearth in the center of the cabin.

LOG CABIN DESIGNS

The Log Cabin quilt shown in no. 38 is set in the Sunshine and Shadows design. The blocks are pieced onto a foundation of coarse muslin and use the pleated technique, where the logs appear to be folded, with none of the seams visible on the top of the quilt. The center square of each block is red wool, symbolic of the fire in the hearth. The remaining narrow strips are challis, a very lightweight wool or cotton and wool fabric, usually printed.

The quilt is finished with a blue challis binding. There is no backing, so all the stitches on the foundation blocks are visible on the back of the quilt. As was common for this type of quilt done on a foundation, no batting or quilting was added. The quilt is quite heavy without it.

39. Log Cabin, c. 1860, Lancaster County, Pennsylvania, 82½ x 83 inches, pieced cottons. (Collection of Jean Christensen)

An unusual strip border adds interest to the Log Cabin quilt shown in no. 39. Made in Lancaster County, Pennsylvania, about 1860, this scrap basket quilt features the popular madder and chocolate (variations of brown) prints along with the double pinks. The color has been skillfully arranged, and the pinks define and organize the design arrangement. Having never been used, the quilt is in excellent condition. It is set in the Barn Raising design, then beautifully framed with a border made from blocks of strips. The minimal quilting was done in a grid pattern. The backing is a chocolate brown print, brought to the front as an edge finish.

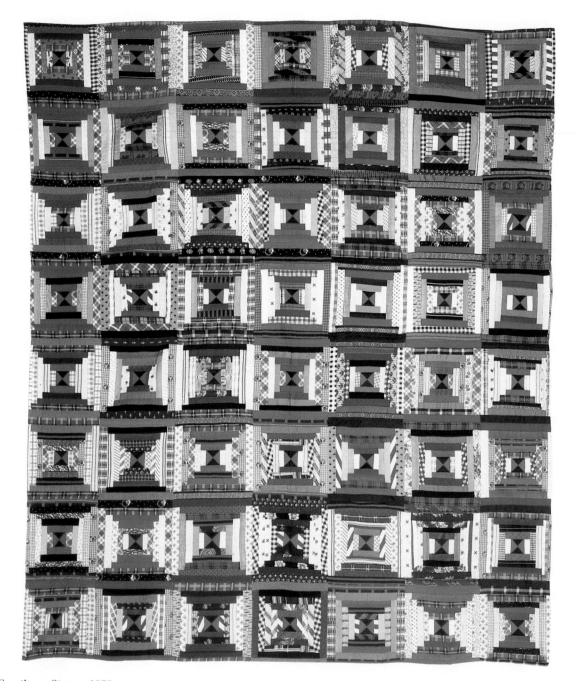

40. Courthouse Steps, c. 1875,
Pennsylvania, 60 x 68 inches,
pieced cottons. (Photo courtesy
of American Hurrah Antiques,
New York City)

COURTHOUSE STEPS

The Courthouse Steps is a variation of the Log Cabin design, with the strips arranged to look like the steps of a building. In some areas it was called White House Steps or Statehouse Steps. The quilt shown in no. 40 is composed of brightly colored strips of cotton and challis, sewn to a foundation. It is unquilted, with the front edges turned to the back as an edge finish. Made by a Mennonite quilter in Pennsylvania, this quilt reflects the exuberant color scheme of the area. The use of white brightens the quilt, and the unusual pieced center squares add interest.

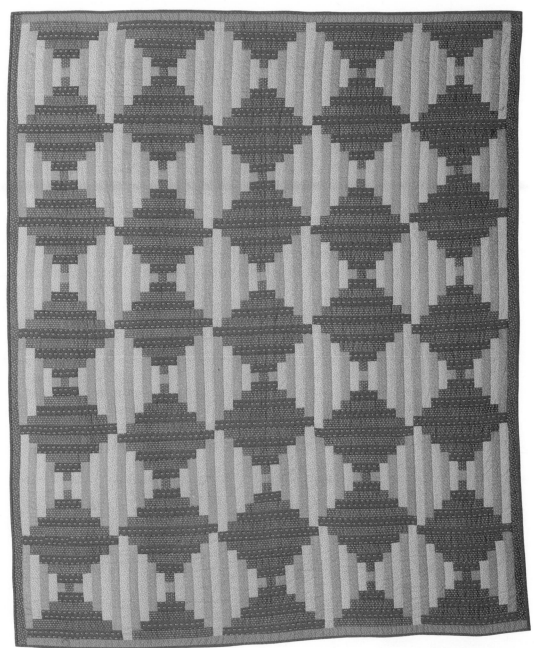

41. Japanese Lanterns, c. 1890,
Berks County, Pennsylvania,
77 x 81 inches, pieced cottons.
(Collection of Nancy J. Martin)

JAPANESE LANTERNS

Another Courthouse Steps variation was called Japanese Lanterns because of its resemblance to these Oriental objects. During the 1876 United States Centennial Exhibition in Philadelphia, the Japanese pavilion created such excitement that Oriental motifs—fans, pagodas, and lanterns—became the rage in design. This influence also extended to quiltmaking patterns, as well as to the designs being printed on fabrics.

The quilt shown in no. 41 was made in Berks County, Pennsylvania, about 1890. The unusual color scheme is typical of this Pennsylvania Dutch (Deutsch or German) area. Chrome yellow and double pink print fabrics make up all the vertical strips, while madder and green print fabrics alternate horizontally to form the lanterns.

STATEHOUSE STEPS

Statehouse Steps, shown in no. 42, is another name for the Courthouse Steps design. Sarah Creighton Bryans and her friend Eliza Boyd made this particularly pleasing quilt in 1890 near Strafford, Chester County, Pennsylvania.

Sarah Creighton Bryans married Thomas Brown on 18 January 1872. Thomas Brown had inherited his parents' farm of seventy-five acres of woodland and farm ground. Sarah and Thomas set up housekeeping in a lovely old farmhouse on the property. The acres of cornfields and hay, along with eggs and meat products from the animals, provided their living. Posts and rails also were cut and sold from the woodland. There was, of course, no plumbing, electricity, or phone, and their life was hard. They had only one child, Anne Hughes Brown, born 15 September 1877.

Sarah Bryans Brown befriended Eliza Boyd, who had recently come from Ireland and was lonely. They became close friends, quilting and weaving together. They wove a blue coverlet and a beautiful cloth for the living-room table. A loom was always set up in the parlour. Friends often gave them material for their quilts, and they stitched their blocks in the dim light of a lantern.

Eliza Boyd came to live with Sarah's daughter, Anne, and her family, when Martha, Anne's second child, was born. Martha Kinsey remembers "that she was our nanny until I went to school. She continued to live with us and we would toddle down to my grand-mother's only ten minutes away and I learned about quilting. They would cut strips but gave me a cardboard square and I cut and placed the pieces, then later sewed them for doll quilts. Nanny lived with us but went to homes as a midwife until she died.

"I have the fondest memories of my grandparents. The haying time and taking lemonade to the workers. Picking the wild flowers. Wading in the creek. Pump-kins and corn in the fall. Gathering chestnuts. So many more, to say nothing of the many hours I spent learning to make quilts and learning about a loom, and the delicious smells of bread baking and apple dumplings."

Although Sarah Bryans Brown and Eliza Boyd used scraps for their quilt, it is a rich collection that shows the variety of fabrics available around 1890. Most of the light background fabrics are shirtings, cambrics, and percales in one or two colors, or black on a white- or cream-colored ground that were available year-round. It is unusual that the double-print chrome yellow prints, which really stand out, were used with

Eliza Boyd

Sara Bryans Brown

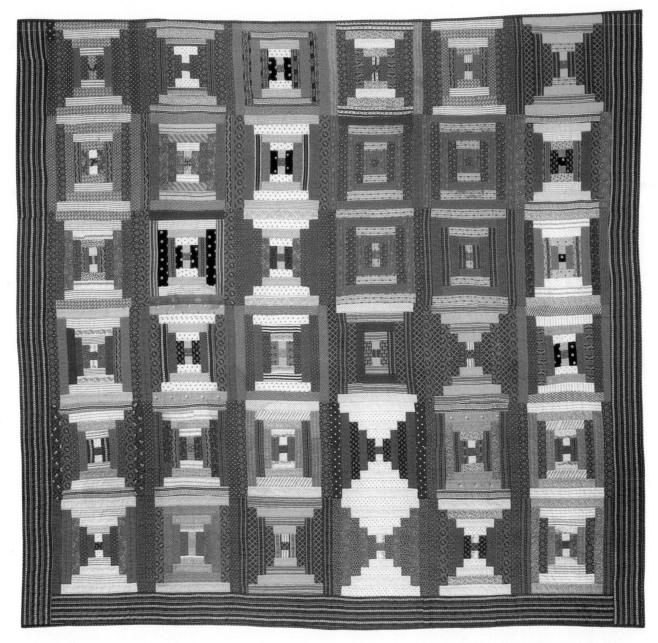

42. Statehouse Steps, c. 1890,
Chester County, Pennsylvania,
86 x 94 inches, pieced cottons.
(Collection of Nancy J. Martin)

the light fabrics. The dark-colored prints are madders or chocolates done on a deep brown ground. Many of the prints appear to be inspired by the designs found on Indian shawls or printed stripes. The border is a striped fabric, used on only three sides of the quilt. One wonders if the top edge was to be covered by a separate bolster or special pillow cases, making the top border unnecessary.

PINEAPPLE

Pineapple designs, another variation of the Log Cabin pattern, became popular in the late nineteenth century. There were many variations and names, including Windmill Blades, Washington's Pavement, and Maltese Cross.

The Pineapple quilt in no. 43 was made by Elizabeth (Lizzy) Wright Sherman about 1910 in Evanston, Illinois. Lizzy was born 6 February 1888 and, although she came from a wealthy family (her grandfather had been mayor of Chicago), she was a thrifty woman who wasted nothing. A real sewing enthusiast, she would spend her evenings stitching. At the end of the evening, she would pull the thread out of her needle and drape it in her hair. She would then wrap the thread around a piece of cardboard so as not to waste it. Her glorious Pineapple quilt combines every con-

43. *Pineapple, c. 1910, Illinois,*
81 x 87 inches, pieced cottons.
(Collection of Sandra N. Wolf)

Elizabeth Wright Sherman

ceivable color and pattern. Lizzy kept the quilt folded at the foot of her bed and used it for "show," rather than sleeping under it.

Before her death in 1963, Lizzy shared her sewing enthusiasm and skills with her great granddaughter, Sandra Wolf, who is the proud owner of the Pineapple quilt.

The Pineapple quilt shown in no. 44 has fewer strips than Lizzy Sherman's quilt, making it a simpler design. Done from solid-color scraps of challis, the blocks are arranged so that color flows across the quilt's surface. The quilt pieces are sewn to a foundation. A backing and separate binding has been added, but this Pineapple design is not quilted.

It is easy to see the Maltese Cross, another name for Pineapple, in this quilt. The solid colors create a strong graphic design, much like those found in the contemporary art quilts of the 1980s.

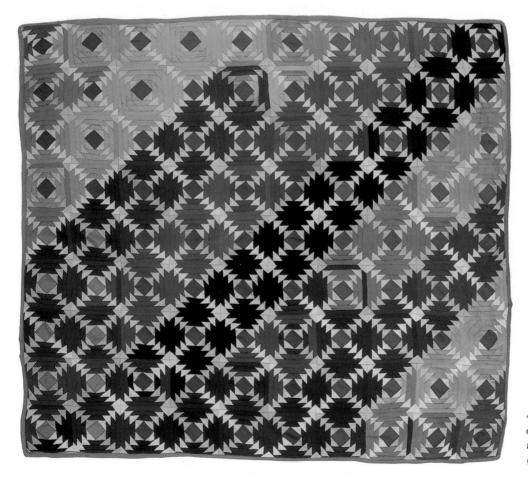

44. Pineapple, c. 1900, origin unknown, 53 x 60 inches, pieced wool challis. (Collection of Luella Doss)

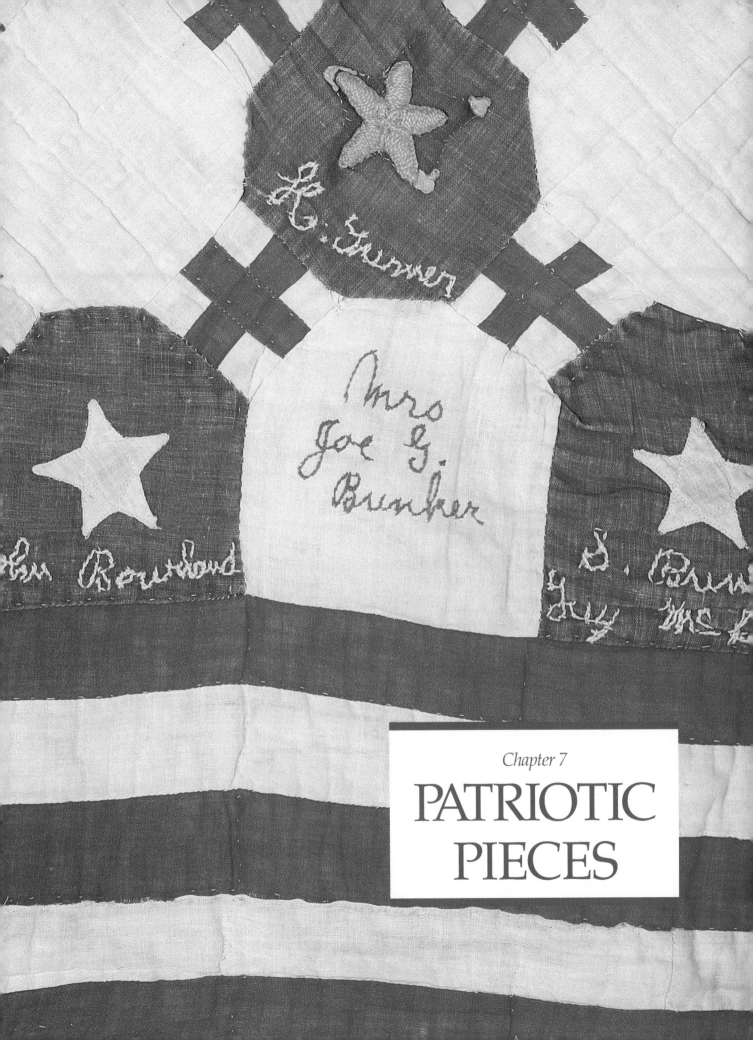

Chapter 7
PATRIOTIC
PIECES

RED, WHITE, AND BLUE

Throughout history, women have created quilts to commemorate important events. Most common are the quilts created to celebrate centennial and bicentennial dates for the founding of a church, organization, town, state, or nation. These patriotic quilts can be the work of one maker, a group effort, or a community project. Some of these quilts remain in the maker's private collection, but most of them are regarded as historical artifacts and are displayed by historical societies and museums.

Many quilts with a patriotic motif were created to raise money for political candidates. Quilts were also raffled to raise funds for schools, churches, and organizations. Often, these quilts took the form of signature quilts. You paid a certain amount of money to sign your name (usually this signature was later embroidered) on a quilt block or square. The fee was determined by both the size and placement of the signature, as well as the prominence of the individual. Businesses usually were charged more, as was anyone whose name was the only one in a square. If your signature shared space with others in a square, the fee was less. You also received a "chance" or ticket to win the quilt in the raffle.

These fund-raising quilts were of several types. Many featured pieced blocks with the signatures on the lighter patches of the block. Others were made with appliqué blocks (Dresden Plate and Sunbonnet Sue were favorites), with the signatures in the background spaces.

Still another variety featured only signatures, with no piecing or appliqué. The arrangement of signatures created the design, most often placed as spokes in a wheel. Sometimes, each "wheel" of signatures contained the same family name in the spokes. Most of these quilts were embroidered in Turkey red thread on a white background, a popular needlework combination.

Red Cross quilts were a specific type of fund-raising quilt that was made after World War I began in 1914. Relief committees, such as the Serbian Distress Fund, actively sought the inclusion of patchwork quilts in packages sent to war-torn Europe.

Many organizations embarked on fund-raising activities to support the Red Cross. In December 1917, *Modern Priscilla* featured an article: "One Thousand Dollars for the Red Cross Can Be Raised on a Memorial Quilt." The article fully explained the procedures necessary to accomplish this goal, including the prices to charge for the squares according to their placement on the quilt top. The organization charged a small sum to embroider names on the quilt, which was then raffled off or auctioned. All monies raised were donated to the Red Cross. The article also showed a model of the ticket form for selling signature blanks. Full pattern instructions included color, yardage, and construction of the quilt.[40]

Another type of patriotic quilt came into being during World War I: the "Liberty Quilt." After the United States entered the war in 1917, the government actively urged its citizens to make quilts, using this slogan in numerous newspaper and magazine ads: MAKE QUILTS—SAVE THE BLANKETS FOR OUR BOYS OVER THERE. In addition, the government had taken the entire "wool clip for the coming year," and factories were not able to make blankets for the civilian population.

Adopting the slogan, *Modern Priscilla* magazine featured an article in the September 1918 issue, "Calling the Quilts into Service for Our Country." Four quilt patterns were offered; one was a design to be quilted on the sewing machine. Numerous utilitarian quilts for home-front use were made in response to the slogan. These quilts, regardless of their actual design, soon earned the nickname "Liberty Quilts."

During the depression, the Works Progress Administration (WPA) sponsored a Federal Art Project program called the Index of American Design. Its purpose was to trace and document in visual form the best of American folk and decorative arts from the seventeenth century to 1900. The project provided training and income for out-of-work artists, who were to produce watercolor renderings of the objects being documented.

Thirty-five states participated in the project, and most of them had a quilt-rendering group. In South Langhorne and Croydon, Pennsylvania, Ruth Finley acted as adviser for quilt patterns and quilting techniques. There were special problems for the artists who worked on the quilt renderings. The large size of the quilt, along with the small size of the details and stitches, were hard to capture on a small-scale watercolor. Some artists solved the problem by sketching a detail next to the whole quilt. Others chose to show how the quilt would appear if folded in quarters.

"Some of the people affiliated with the Index as artists, project directors, cooperative lenders, or supporters are names we recognize as being important in twentieth-century quilt history, such as Suzanne Chapman of the Museum of Fine Arts in Boston, Frances Lichten of Pennsylvania, Mrs. Danner, Suzanne Roy, and Florence Peto.

"Unfortunately, because they were incomplete at the advent of World War II, none of the portfolios went into the Index. Nonetheless, the vast accumulation of valuable material in the Index, is now stored at the National Gallery of Art, Washington, D.C."[41]

PATRIOTIC QUILTS

One of the most interesting patriotic quilts is shown in no. 46. It was made by Mrs. Emma Van Fleet in 1866, one year after the end of the Civil War, to commemorate the battles in which her husband fought. According to the names and dates recorded on the quilt, Sergeant Alfred A. Van Fleet of the Illinois State Cavalry Company was engaged in forty-seven Civil War battles. The quilt was inherited by Harvey Hunt, Alfred Van Fleet's grandson, and donated to the Yakima Valley Museum.

46. Patriotic, 1866, Illinois, 66 x 80 inches, pieced and appliquéd cottons with embroidery. (Collection of the Yakima Valley Historical Society)

SIGNATURE CELEBRATIONS

The signature quilt shown in no. 47 is unusual in that it contains the names of two presidents, Benjamin Harrison and Grover Cleveland. Purchased in Illinois, the quilt does not have an inscription block of an organization or any clue as to its purpose. Each signature is accompanied by the name of a town and state. Most of the towns are located in Illinois and Kentucky. The quilt is signed with Benjamin Harrison's address as Washington, D.C., obviously referring to his term as president from 1889 to 1893. Grover Cleveland's address is listed as Buffalo, New York.

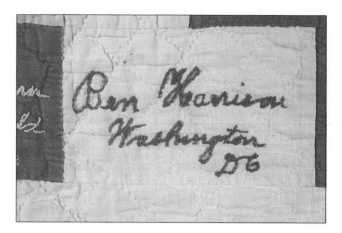

Embroidered signature of
Benjamin Harrison

47. Fund Raising Quilt, c. 1890,
origin unknown, 78 x 82 inches,
pieced cotton with embroidery.
(Collection of Jean Christensen)

*Embroidered signature of
Grover Cleveland*

Interviews by Woodinville, Washington Historical Society members with early pioneers of that area indicate that quilt auctions or raffles of signature quilts were often part of a church social. Ida Jacklin remembers "the pie socials at Mrs. Durham's house, where Japanese lanterns hung in the trees over the tables. At one of these events, a Fourth of July, the Ladies Aid auctioned off a quilt they had made. The quilt, done in red-white-and-blue squares, was full of Woodinville names, each person having paid ten cents to have their name on the quilt."

Cleveland was elected mayor of Buffalo in 1881, and he was governor of New York from 1882 to 1884, prior to his first term as president from 1885 to 1889. Although Cleveland had more popular votes, Harrison received more electoral votes to win the election of 1888. Cleveland then defeated Harrison in the election of 1892 and served from 1893 to 1897. So, Cleveland could have been in Buffalo in the 1889–93 period, but his official biography states that he moved to New York City at the end of his first term and returned to the practice of law. The quilt is also signed by Cleveland's niece, Miss Ruth Cleveland of New York City, who may have been the maker of the quilt.

Ladies Aid societies often made signature quilts as fund raisers. The quilt pictured in no. 48 was made in 1902 by the Ladies Aid Society of the First Baptist Church of North Yakima, Washington. Each woman was given a block and was responsible for getting ten names at ten cents a name. Several blocks had more than ten names. The maker of the block could arrange the names in her own design, so wheels, ladders, stars, leaves, and umbrellas were constructed from the signatures. One block was sent to Southbury Baptist Church in Connecticut and another to the First Baptist Church in Berlin, Wisconsin.

The quilt was then raffled off at ten cents a ticket, and having your name on the quilt did not include a chance to win the quilt. It was won by Mrs. Emma Dunning, who bequeathed the quilt to Leslie Morgan, a classmate in her Sunday School class at the time the quilt was made.

*48. Ladies Aid Quilt, 1902,
Washington, 57½ x 73 inches,
pieced cotton with embroidery.
(Private collection)*

The bicentennial quilt made by Marjorie Meyers, shown in no. 49, contains signatures of all the state governors who were in office in 1976, along with the president of the United States. Marjorie decided to use the St. Andrew's Cross pattern. She mailed a piece of white fabric to each governor and President Gerald Ford, asking them to sign their names. All the fabrics were returned, including one with a rubber-stamped signature!

Marjorie's planning and symbolism are typical of quilters' commemorative designs. "Back in 1975, I decided that I wanted to make a quilt to celebrate the bicentennial year in 1976. I've always had an interest in quilts and had just started making them. To me, the colors were to be red, white, and blue. Also, I wanted to incorporate in some way the name of each state, its capital, and the year it became a part of the Union. Thoughts were racing around in my head for a design that could put all these facts together. One day I thought of a square with strips running from diagonal corner to diagonal corner, with a small square on a point in the center. I thought I had a new pattern, then I found it in *American Quilts and How to Make Them* by Carter Houck and Myron Miller, listed as St. Andrew's Cross.

"Then I remembered thinking, 'Why not get each governor's signature on that last piece of fabric.' I found a blue background fabric with stars on it and saw the same fabric in red.

"Fall came and it was time to get children off to school, then the holidays with all the business that goes with them. So, in January, I knew I had to get busy or my goal of having the quilt done by the Fourth of July wouldn't come about. I sent each governor a letter and asked them to sign the enclosed piece of fabric.

"By the middle of February, all requests had been sent off. I started embroidering on the pieces of fabric that I had already prepared. I also had to figure out how I was going to set these blocks together. I finally decided on six blocks across and nine down. That gave me an extra four blocks. I'd already planned on putting the states down in order by date going from left to right. So on one block, I wrote "Happy Birthday United States of America." For another block, I wrote to our president, Gerald Ford, and asked for his signature. That left two empty blocks, which would serve as spacers.

"Signatures started coming in within a week or so of being sent. Finally, the top was done, the backing was ready, and it was time to quilt. This was really one of my first big quilts, so the need to hurry did not help in the size of my quilting stitches, but I did finish the end of June."

Marjorie, born 25 January 1939, lives in Bothell, Washington, and enjoys making all types of quilts. She married Merle Meyers on 20 March 1956. They have five children and eight grandchildren, all of whom have received special quilts from this lady. Margie strongly believes in making special quilts for special occasions. For their thirtieth anniversary, she presented Merle with a quilt featuring thirty hearts.

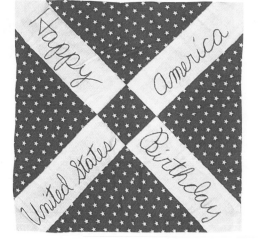 

Inscription blocks

49. Bicentennial Quilt, 1976,
Washington, 88 x 112 inches,
pieced cotton with embroidery.
(Private collection)

Red Cross Relief

The Stanwood Ladies Aid Society of Our Savior's Lutheran Church in Stanwood, Washington, made the quilt shown in no. 50 in 1918 to help with the Red Cross relief work. The quilt consists of seventy-six blocks, each eight inches square, on which eight signatures radiate from a center circle like spokes from a wheel. The circle and signatures are embroidered in what appears to be pink embroidery floss. However, since the fabric is discolored near the signatures, this floss was probably a Turkey red that was not colorfast.

In the center of the quilt, a legend has been embroidered along with flags and a colorful shield. The embroidery, done in a variegated gold floss, reads: "Stanwood Ladies Aid, Old Savior's Church, 1918." The flags are those of France, the United States, Great Britain, Belgium, and the American Red Cross.

Inscription block

*50. Red Cross Quilt, 1918,
Washington, 66 x 72 inches,
pieced cotton with embroidery.
(Private collection)*

In 1919, Mrs. G. W. Moore made a quilt (no. 51), along with the members of the Red Cross Guild in Equality, Illinois. Martha Moore did not quilt as a rule. Martha had several children, but only one daughter, Zerita, who was the "pet" of the family. She was seldom referred to by her given name; instead she was called "Pet." Martha was quite proud of her work and signed her name, age, and date in the corner: "Pieced by Mrs. G. W. Moore, age 71 — 1919."

Martha included the names of her children and grandchildren on her quilt, including Zerita Moore and then again with Zerita's married name, Mrs. C. W. Turner, and her grandson, Charles W. Turner II.

Upon close examination, you will see the area near the border contains many names, sometimes more than once. The name "C. Nation" is on one of the blue blocks with a white star. Speculation has been made that this might be early suffragette Carrie Nation. However, Carrie Nation died in 1911. Another interesting inscrip-

tion reads "Arthur Smith — Bond Boy."

The quilt itself is composed of blue octagonal pieces with white octagonal pieces and small squares containing a red cross. The Octagon pattern was probably used to construct the quilt. Other early names for this pattern were Job's Trouble, Mechanical Blocks, Snowballs, and Ozark Cobblestones. A white star has been sewn by machine to each blue piece that touches the border. Gold stars were stitched with heavy perle cotton onto a satin star near each corner. The satin has deteriorated, but the gold embroidery remains.

A six-inch-wide striped border surrounds the quilt on four sides. Five white stars are machine stitched to a field of blue in each corner. A printed fabric, which was probably intended for shirting, forms the backing. Both the front and back edges have been folded to the inside and secured with a blanket stitch done in perle cotton, a very unusual edge finish.

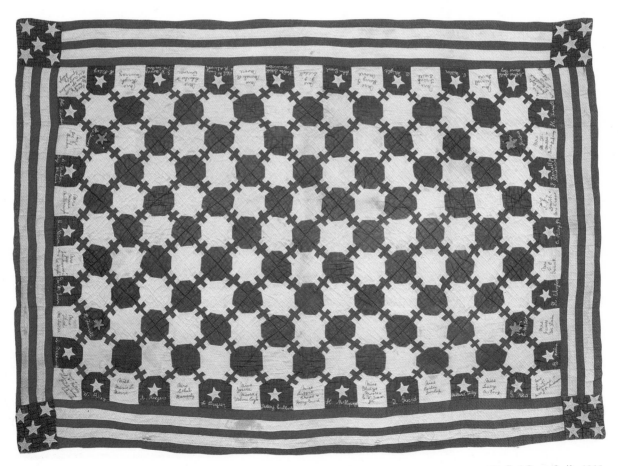

51. Red Cross Quilt, 1919, Illinois, 60 x 80 inches, pieced cotton with embroidery. (Private collection)

WORLD WAR II INSPIRATIONS

World War II also inspired quilts. *Ladies' Home Journal* offered the "War Brides Quilt" and the "Navy Wives Quilt." The Mountain Mist Pattern Company (now Stearns Technical Textiles) designed two patterns for their readers: Sea Wings to Glory, featuring the Navy emblem (no. 52) and Wings over All, featuring the Army emblem (no. 53). These patterns are still offered in their catalog because of the "numerous requests from mothers of boys in the Air Corps during the Second World War. Although this is a 'dated' design it is still very popular with mothers of young men in Service. It is also popular with mothers of small boys for use in their bedrooms."[42]

The *Kansas City Star* printed two wartime patterns in 1943. The first was a tribute to the Red Cross, printed 7 April 1943. The second, printed 26 May 1943, was contributed by two young men, Eugene Aubuchan and Earl J. Payton, in an army training camp, in appreciation for the many thoughtful deeds American women had done for soldiers.

53. Army emblem from center section of Wings over All, 1942, origin unknown, 80 x 96 inches, pieced and appliquéd cottons. This quilt is essentially the same as no. 52 except for the center emblem. (Collection of the Stearns and Foster Company)

52. Sea Wings to Glory, 1943, origin unknown, 80 x 96 inches, pieced and appliquéd cottons. (Collection of the Stearns and Foster Company)

Y KANSAS CITY STAR, WEDNESDAY, APRIL 7, 1943.

SALUTE TO LOYALTY.

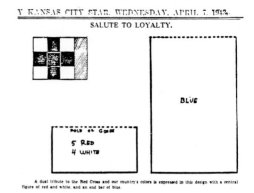

Wartime patterns from the
Kansas City Star

A dual tribute to the Red Cross and our country's colors is expressed in this design with a central figure of red and white, and an end bar of blue.

THE ARMY STAR.

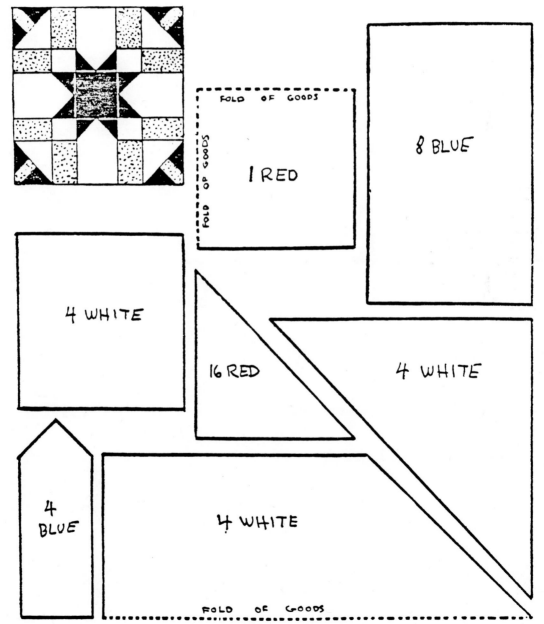

In appreciation of the many thoughtful deeds of American women for soldiers, two young men in an army training camp have sent The Weekly Star this pattern of their own origination. They are Eugene Aubuchan and Earl J Faxton. Their addresses may not be revealed. Red. white and blue are the colors they chose for the design. They also suggest placing a white strip across the top of the quilt and stitching on it the letters "U. S. A."

Chapter 8

POPULAR
PASTELS

*Newspaper clippings and a pattern
from the thirties*

Women's magazines also featured regular articles on quilting. Ann Orr, whose quilt designs were composed of small squares reminiscent of her earlier cross-stitch and filet crochet work, became art-needlework editor of *Good Housekeeping* magazine. She contributed a page a month until her retirement in 1940. Readers' orders were referred to the Ann Orr Studio in Nashville, Tennessee.

From the influential women's periodical *Ladies' Home Journal* emerged some of the most distinguished writer-researchers of the period. They were Mrs. Leopold Simon, Elizabeth Daingerfield, and Marie D. Webster.

Marie D. Webster's quilt designs appeared in *Ladies' Home Journal* and *Ladies' Home Journal Embroidery Book* from 1911 to 1915. The majority of these designs were her originals, and a few were her adaptations of old patterns. "Her designing talent was so prodigious that today we can say without a fear of contradiction that Marie Webster has been the single 'most copied' quilt designer in the twentieth century."[47]

As mentioned earlier, farm women were the mainstay of quiltmaking during the 1920s and 1930s. They eagerly awaited the arrival of *Farm and Fireside, Rural Progress, Ohio Farmer, Orange Judd Farmer, National Stockman and Farmer,* and *Hearth and Home,* all of which contained quilting columns.

The twentieth century was also the first era when books solely devoted to quilting were published, the landmark volume being Marie D. Webster's *Quilts: Their Story and How to Make Them* (1915), which included color plates of quilts she had designed while she was needlework editor at *Ladies' Home Journal.*

In 1929 Ruth Finley's *Old Patchwork Quilts* covered the making of quilts, the origins of quilt names, and even the migration of patterns. Ruby McKim's *101 Patchwork Patterns* (1931) is still in print today. Carrie Hall and Rose Kretsinger broke new ground with their *Romance of the Patchwork Quilt in America* (1933), which contained Mrs. Hall's 800 different quilt blocks, a source for pattern identification that remains invaluable. Florence Peto further filled in the quilt picture with *Historic Quilts* in 1939 and *American Quilts and Coverlets* in 1949. In 1946 Dr. William Rush Dunton's *Old Quilts* offered his theory that quilting was excellent occupational therapy for "nervous ladies" and which impressively documented the "Baltimore Album" quilt.[48]

MAIL ORDER

Mail-order companies were a popular pattern resource during this period. The largest was the Ladies Art Company of St. Louis, which published *Diagrams of Quilt Sofa and Pin Cushion Patterns.*

The company claimed that by the 1920s, their mail-order business employed fifty people. There were undoubtedly other companies who may have sold patterns in a limited area, but Ladies Art from the beginning must have intended to go national, since they ran ads for their catalog in *Good Housekeeping.* In about 1910, the *Catalog of Practical Needlework—Quilt Patterns,* by Clara A. Stone, offered 186 traditional quilt patterns. This catalog appears to be an outgrowth of her contributions to *Hearth and Home* and has a New England-East Coast orientation to the pattern names.[49]

Then, as today, the leading designers of quilt patterns were held in high regard by the quilters of America. When a woman saw a quilt made by Ann Orr or Marie Webster, she wanted to make that particular quilt exactly like the original. Many of the leading quilt designers and columnists of the day ran a reader service or mail-order business. They also offered kits for their quilts, although these were never as popular as the patterns.

Marie Webster, *Ladies' Home Journal* needlework editor from 1911 to 1917, operated a pattern and kit business from her home in Marion, Indiana. Ann Orr, *Good Housekeeping*'s art-needlework editor from 1919 to 1940, ran an extensive pattern and kit business from her home in Nashville, Tennessee. Rose Kretsinger, coauthor of *The Romance of the Patchwork Quilt in America,* freely shared her patterns for years, then finally began selling them. Carlie Sexton Holmes, who was a contributor to *Better Homes and Gardens* as well as a number of farm journals, ran a pattern business in Des Moines, Iowa. Ruby McKim, the original pattern illustrator for the *Kansas City Star,* sold her patterns through the McKim Studios.

Reader service bureaus were run by newspapers and magazines which featured quilting columns. Many of these periodicals, such as *Ladies' Home Journal, Good Housekeeping,* and the *Kansas City Star,* relied on their needlework editors, who also ran pattern businesses, to serve as the fulfillment service for patterns and kits.

But often, the needlework editor responsible had no experience or interest in quilting and patchwork. These editors could best satisfy their readers' demand for patterns by using the services of a syndicated pattern company. The Home Arts syndicate offered the pattern line of Bettina, Hope Winslow, and Colonial Quilts, while the Laura Wheeler and Alice Brooks patterns were offered by the Old Chelsea Station Needlecraft Service syndicate.

Batting companies were also responsible for supplying patterns to quilters. They helped the quilting revival by sponsoring contests and printing patterns on the inside of the batting wrapper. One company, the Rock River Cotton Company, offered a full-sized roll of their Crown batting free to anyone sending in ten Crown Jewel trademarks cut from wrappers.

The Stearns and Foster Company, a batting producer dating back to 1846, has sponsored many projects to promote quilting and preserve its history. They began printing patterns on the inside of their batting wrappers in 1929. In the 1920s and 1930s, serious quilters nationwide were commissioned to develop new patterns based on traditional favorites. These quilts were exhibited in store windows and displays to promote and advertise quiltmaking. Then, in 1949, Stearns and Foster sponsored the Central States Quilt Exhibition, which consisted of prize-winning quilts from state fairs.

Stearns and Foster marketed their batting under the name of Mountain Mist. Today, under the name of Stearns Technical Textiles, they still print a pattern on the inside of the batting wrapper and also sell these same patterns (there are 129 in all) through their catalog.

KITS FOR QUILTS

The sale of quilting patterns proliferated freely during the 1930s. However, kits were considered a controversial item. Women were beginning to view quilting as an art and disliked the "paint-by-number" approach of the kits, even though they were offered for sale by such prestigious magazines as *Good Housekeeping* and *Ladies' Home Journal* and were created by popular designers such as Marie Webster and Anne Orr. *Modern Priscilla* magazine even used the kits as a subscription incentive.

Beginning in 1898, the Ladies Art Company catalog offered blocks and finished items. Presewn quilt blocks could be ordered for 35 cents to $1.50, and the price for a complete quilt ranged from $25 to $45, depending on the complexity of the pattern. In 1922 they offered a stamped kit for $5.

Quilt kits were time-savers only in design planning and the choosing and buying of fabrics. Even with a kit there was much work to be done. The designs had to be stamped by hand, using a perforated paper pattern and a rubbing stamp powder (usually blue or yellow).

Kits became more popular with the advent of iron-on transfers and prestamped fabrics. Paragon and Herrschners were companies that supplied a wide variety of prestamped quilting kits.

In later years, these kits contained a 90-by-104-inch percale sheet with the appliqué and embroidered placement already stamped, plus fabric and thread for the appliqué and finishing details. Even the quilting design was stamped on the fabric. It is easy to see why a creative and ambitious quilter would have found these kits stifling, but these carefully structured kits appealed to inexperienced quiltmakers or those who were too inhibited to devise their own designs.

END OF THE REVIVAL

Despite the patriotic quilts made during World War II, quilting was past its peak when the war began. Several factors were responsible for this.

First, thousands of women were recruited into the wartime labor force to work in factories and to fill men's jobs in other fields, in addition to running their homes. Obviously, their free time became minimal. Second, fabric became scarcer and more expensive. Pattern companies also had to struggle with the rising cost of paper. Many leading figures in quiltmaking and pattern design turned to other pursuits: Ruby McKim to dolls and Carrie Hall to fashion, for example.

When Americans came back from the war, it was a very different era. The modern age had become the atomic age. Women's interests turned to babies, mortgages, fin-tailed cars, television, and all the diversions that postwar prosperity had to offer. In the fifties, the shape of the times was modern—from the inexpensive plywood furniture pioneered by Charles Eames to the kidney-shaped coffee tables and "prefab" suburban houses. The whole point of fifties design was not to re-create an early, antique, Colonial era but to forge ahead and shape familiar objects anew. Even fabrics became man-made. Dacron was introduced by DuPont in 1951, about the time acrylic was unveiled. Lightweight and wrinkle-proof, it seemed as if it and the earlier nylon and rayon would supplant cotton in clothing. However, these synthetics were uninspiring to quilters.[50]

Although quilts continued to be made by some women, the quilting revival had become a thing of the past.

BROKEN STAR

The Broken Star quilt, made by Arlie Byrd Janssen for her daughter Arlene (no. 54), shows the predominantly pastel color palette used by thirties' quilters. Arlie made many quilts in the thirties, all of them from popular designs of the day: Flower Garden, Wedding Ring, Butterfly, and Sunbonnet Sue. Her daughter, Arlene B. Giegling, recalls, "There was always a quilt up in her home, a neighbor's, or the church basement. If they quilted a quilt for anyone, they charged so much per spool of thread and gave the money to the Ladies Aid."

Arlie was born on 22 February 1894 on a farm near Masena, Iowa. She was the oldest of six girls and four boys. The family was of Scotch, English, Irish, and Pennsylvania Dutch descent, a "mixed Yankee" according to her mother-in-law.

When she was seventeen, Arlie married B. E. Janssen on 7 June 1911. They lived in the small town of Emery, South Dakota, for over fifty-one years. She had three daughters but lost her middle child during the flu epidemic of 1918.

Arlie took an active part in the U. P. W. of the

B. E. and Arlie Janssen

Presbyterian Church and the church itself. Her beautiful handwork was always sought after at bazaars or fund raisers: quilts or comforters made from woolen suit samples, embroidered and lace pillow cases and sheets, and fancy tea towels made from bleached flour sacks. Her food items, chocolate angel food cake and apple pies, were also prized at the bazaars. She took great care in feeding the cookstove just the right amount of dry corncobs and kindling to maintain the proper temperature for the cakes.

The Broken Star quilt is finely quilted inside each diamond shape and features decorative quilting inside each larger white area. There is a solid-color "thirties' green" backing, with a separate binding as an edge finish.

54. *Broken Star, 1932, South Dakota,*
76 x 78 inches, pieced cottons.
(Collection of Nancy J. Martin)

HONEYMOON COTTAGE

Pieced picture quilts depicting houses began to make an appearance in the late 1800s and enjoyed special popularity in the 1890s and again in the 1930s. Honeymoon Cottage was designed by Ruby Short McKim in 1930. It was available as a mail-order pattern from Sears, Roebuck & Co. and was described by the designer: "The Honeymoon Cottage has a quaint, old-fashioned charm that will appeal to all lovers of a squat, broad-eaved, little home with wide, hospitable doorway and fireplace."[51]

The red and green version of this pattern, shown in no. 55, reflects a popular color scheme of the time. Bungalows were as familiar to twentieth-century quilters as the log cabin was to their ancestors.

The bungalows are quilted with a grid pattern. The 2½-inch-wide borders between the bungalows are filled with elaborate feather quilting. The quilt is bound with strips of red fabric.

55. Honeymoon Cottage, c. 1935,
origin unknown, 72 x 76 inches,
pieced cottons. (Collection of
Nancy J. Martin)

LONE STAR

The Lone Star shown in no. 56 was purchased at the estate sale of Mrs. Edith Mae Hinton in Scottsville, Kentucky, on 1 March 1986. Edith Mae was a retired school teacher who taught many years in a one-room country school in Pleasant Ridge, Kentucky. She enjoyed quiltmaking and made many quilts. Edith was born 8 May 1902 and married Enzie Hinton on 27 November 1927. Hinton was both her maiden and married name. She died 18 January 1988. Edith enjoyed fancy linens and also had a collection of handmade lace. The Lone Star design shown here has been hand pieced in a marvelous collection of thirties' pastel prints and accented by a strong turquoise solid and an equally strong burgundy print. Since there is little contrast in thirties' prints, they often seem to run together. However, in this quilt, the two strong colors help give definition to the quilt's center, preventing it from appearing soft and "grainy." A solid "thirties' green" serves as a background for these lively prints.

Most unusual is the shape of the quilt, which was obviously made for a single bed. Rather than scale down the design so that the entire star motif would fit across the quilt's width, Edith Mae merely chopped off the side tips of the star.

The quilt is exquisitely quilted with tiny, even stitches in a grid design on the solid green and in an outline of each diamond. A coarse, lighter green fabric has been used for the backing, and a separate binding of the solid green has been done by hand.

The Lone Star quilt design has been a favorite of quiltmakers through the years. For another version of a Lone Star quilt and a brief history of this design, see pages 11–12.

56. Lone Star, c. 1935, Kentucky,
64 x 74 inches, pieced cottons.
(Collection of Nancy J. Martin)

BARBARA FRIETCHIE STAR

The quilt shown in no. 57 is alleged to have been made by the Edith Mae Hinton who also made the Lone Star quilt in no. 56. Purchased at the estate sale of Mrs. Hinton in Scottsville, Kentucky, in 1986, this is a scrap quilt full of exuberant fabrics of many colors: bright watermelon pink, peach, or a tawny brown solid for some of the stars; striped shirtings, dots, plaids, or printed dress goods for the background; and a lively blue-and-white polka dot for the sashing. It is typical of the relaxed attitude quilters displayed in the 1930s, when a myriad of patterned fabrics was available at an inexpensive price. Also known as Pieced Star and Star Puzzle, this pattern is called Barbara Frietchie Star according to a Grandmother Clark pattern published in 1932. The origin of the name is unclear, although Barbara Frietchie is the heroine of the noted poem by John G. Whittier. The poem is based on a story first published in the *Atlantic Monthly* in 1863. According to the story, the men of Frederick, Maryland, hauled down the flag as Confederate troops under Stonewall Jackson's command approached. But Barbara Frietchie supposedly set it in her window. She then seized the flag as bullets ripped through it and proclaimed to the soldiers (according to Whittier's poem): " 'Shoot, if you must, this old grayhead, But spare your country's flag,' she said." A tablet marks the spot where this incident is said to have occurred.

The quilt is quilted in a widely spaced rainbow or Baptist Fan pattern, often used on utility quilts. A very coarse muslin is used for the backing, and on three sides of the quilt this backing is turned to the front and used as an edge finish. On the remaining side of the quilt, the raw edges are folded to the inside, then loosely stitched together.

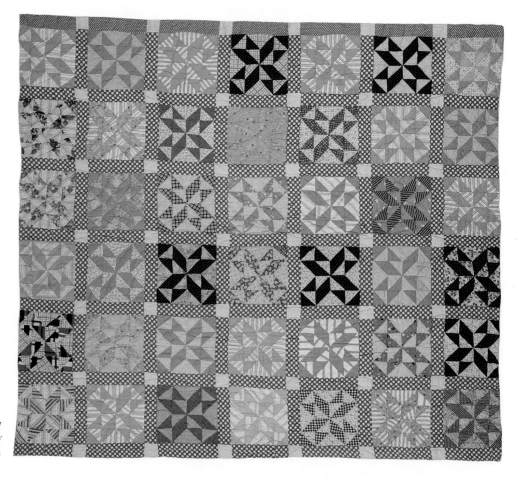

57. Barbara Frietchie Star, c. 1935, Kentucky, 70 x 81 inches, pieced cottons. (Collection of Nancy J. Martin)

Maple Leaf

The Maple Leaf quilt shown in no. 58 typifies the thirties' penchant for pastel color schemes, regardless of the more common autumn colors usually chosen for this block. The fabric is sateen, a fashionable fabric in the 1930s. Sateen was a loosely woven cotton fabric with a glossy surface meant to resemble satin. An unknown quiltmaker pieced the sixty-one nine-inch Maple Leaf blocks for this quilt by hand. The Maple Leaf stems are hand appliquéd. The Maple Leaf blocks are sewn together in a diagonal set so that all the motifs face up (or if you prefer, down, as if they were falling).

Pink sateen fills in the empty spaces and completes the quilt's rectangular shape. This top was quilted at a later date.

The green in the color scheme is often referred to as "thirties' green." It is a grayed pastel green that was called "Nile green" in the 1927 catalog from Sears, Roebuck & Co. It is a unique color, almost impossible to find today, but it was the mainstay of many thirties' quilts. Referred to by other regional names, this shade has also been called "Paris green," "institutional green," "arsenic green," and "depression green."

58. Maple Leaf, c. 1935, origin unknown, 75 x 80 inches, pieced cottons. (Collection of Nancy J. Martin)

Appliqué Poppy

Quilt patterns and kits were readily available during the 1930s. Many mail-order businesses sprang up in homes or small shops. When Grace Koenig saw a picture in a library book of the Poppy quilt designed by Marie Webster (1922), she wrote to the author and ordered the pattern. Grace made three of these Poppy quilts (one is shown in no. 59), keeping one and giving the other two away.

Grace used pink and rose fabrics in her Oriental Poppy quilt, pink being her favorite color. Her first memory is of holding a fragile, pink glass Christmas ornament. "It was a bird with a white tail and wings. Mother was admonishing me not to squeeze it, as she sat and sewed on her Singer sewing machine and I sat on the floor by her feet. Of course, in my eagerness to show that bird how much I loved it, I did break it (the only tree ornament that we had)."

Grace Koenig was born in 1895 and grew up in the small mill town of McMurray, Washington. McMurray was a typical small town with a general store, owned and operated by the lumber company; a post office; a meat market; a barber shop; and another grocery with the town's meeting room on the second floor.

"The schoolhouse and the church were the center of any social life the town enjoyed. There were oyster suppers and strawberry socials in season—all the 'fixins' had to be shipped in so they only happened about once a year. A tall Christmas tree that reached to the rafters was decorated in either the school or the church and was trimmed with cotton from batting, and real, lighted candles. No one ever considered fire. Gifts for the children, one each with hard candy and nuts, were purchased by every family and bachelor in town."

No one taught Grace how to piece or quilt, but her family had always made quilts from scraps to use as bedcovers. Grace suffered a lapse in her health in the late 1920s, confining her to a wheelchair or requiring her to use a cane for over seven years. She looked for something to do with her hands to fill the time. She acquired a roll of cotton (a quilt batt) and found the pattern for a Dresden Plate quilt inside.

She used this pattern to make her first quilt, piecing it from fabric she found in a piece bag. The family piece bag was a one-hundred-pound flour sack containing every scrap saved from home sewing. The Dresden Plate quilt later won first prize at the Western Washington Fair in Puyallup. This quilt now belongs to Grace's grandson.

Grace has made many quilts in her lifetime and continues to enjoy quilting at the age of 94. She appreciates all types of needlework and comments on the dress she is wearing in the photo, "It was made of sheer voile and worn over a white taffeta slip. It had French embroidery and punchwork and was made by me especially for my wedding. I kept it in a 'hope' chest."

Grace Koenig and child (1912)

59. *Appliqué Poppy, 1935,*
Washington, 84 x 94 inches,
pieced cottons. (Private collection)

EMBROIDERY QUILT

The embroidered quilt shown in no. 60 is typical of the many children's quilts made during this period. Each seven-inch-square block has been embroidered with what must have been Turkey red floss. Many of the blocks relate to a children's theme, with children dressed in old-fashioned rompers, ruffled dresses, pantaloons, and bonnets. The blocks were stitched together, and then the seams were covered with embroidery. A narrow red border and a wider white border, both quilted with cables, surround the embroidered blocks, which are quilted with an overall grid. The quilt is bound with a commercially made bias tape (probably of a later vintage), which has been carelessly stitched by machine.

Young children often learned their alphabet or animal names from blocks like those shown below. The Valley Supply Company in St. Louis, Missouri, offered several series of pictorial theme blocks: animals, toys, nursery rhymes, and folk tales.

60. Embroidery Quilt, c. 1935,
Maryland, 75 x 76 inches, pieced
and embroidered cottons.
(Collection of Nancy J. Martin)

Chapter 9

QUILTING CLASSICS

61. Oak Leaf Medallion with Sawtooth Borders, c. 1865, Binghamton, New York, 72¼ x 73¼ inches, pieced cottons. (Collection of Jean Christensen)

ENDURING INTEREST

Webster defines "classic" as "having recognized and permanent value: of enduring interest and appeal." "Classic" also refers to a design that has become a standard. Certainly, the Oak Leaf Medallion, Tree of Life, Puss in a Corner, and Burgoyne Surrounded patterns are considered classics. All are patterns that have been faithfully used over the years.

The color schemes of these quilts are classic—red and green, which was popular from the midnineteenth century on, and Turkey red or indigo blue with white. Patricia Mainardi in *Quilts: The Great American Art* explains why women chose these fabrics: "Even in their choice of material, women quiltmakers behaved similarly to other artists. They wanted to use only the most permanent materials, and the popularity of two colors, indigo and Turkey red (an alizarin dye), was the result of their ability to withstand much use without fading."[52]

The quilts shown in this section span a long period of time, but because of their classic design and color schemes, a classic quilt made in 1989 will strongly resemble a classic quilt made in 1850. Any of these quilts can be reproduced in the traditional manner, using hand piecing and hand quilting. However, you can also use the timesaving Template-Free™ methods given on pages 130–135. Using modern tools and technology (a sewing machine, rotary cutter, and Bias Square™ will speed you through the piecing process and allow you to spend more time on the lavish hand quilting.

Elaborate hand quilting is one of the hallmarks of a classic quilt. The white spaces left in these designs serve as a perfect background for traditional hand quilting designs: grids, cables, feathers, and hearts.

OAK LEAF MEDALLION WITH SAWTOOTH BORDERS

Adelade Johnson made the magnificent Oak Leaf Medallion with Sawtooth Borders, shown in no. 61, in Binghamton, New York, in 1865. She used navy-and-white polka-dot fabric against a white background to achieve the strong contrasts that are emphasized by the Sawtooth borders. The hand appliquéd Oak Leaf center adds graceful curves, which help to soften this angular design. The white areas of the quilt are heavily quilted in a "hanging-diamonds" pattern. This was often used on older quilts as a "filler" design when quilting large areas. Adelade used a white solid fabric for the backing. The quilt is bound with a separate binding of the blue-and-white polka-dot fabric.

Sawtooth designs and borders were common in early quilts. According to Ruth Finley, "Probably the most commonly used pieced borders were the Saw Tooth and the Double Saw Tooth."[53]

Saws were an ever-present symbol of pioneer life during the early years of our country. As people moved westward into unsettled areas, they used the saw to clear the land for homes and farms.

The appliquéd Oak Leaf center may also be symbolic, for the oak stood for steadfastness, and Oak Leaf designs were often used in friendship quilts.

TREE OF LIFE

The Tree of Life pattern, symbolic of good luck and renewed or everlasting life, has long been a quilter's favorite. The pine tree itself is an old design used in colonial New England on coins and flags. The name and structure of the block encountered regional changes as pioneer families moved across the country. Most often the name, Tree of Life, refers to a religious context as it is found in the Book of Revelations,

"Blessed are they that do His commandments that they may have right to the tree of life, and may enter in through the gates into the city." (Rev. 22:14)

The Tree of Life quilt shown in no. 62 is done in a red-and-green color scheme. Although the maker of this quilt is unknown, it has the primitive look of a utility quilt. The straight set blocks, absence of lattice and borders, and broad tree trunks all contribute to a naive but pleasing look.

62. Tree of Life, c. 1865–1875, origin unknown, 74 x 82 inches, pieced cottons. (Collection of Great Expectations)

Puss in a Corner

Puss in a Corner, a variation of the Ninepatch design, is a very old block. In Marie Webster's *Quilts: Their Story and How to Make Them,* there is a photograph of a diagonally set Puss in a Corner quilt made in 1855.

Young girls learned to stitch using the Ninepatch and Puss in a Corner designs because they were easy to construct. The Puss in a Corner design makes a good linking block and is often set together with alternate plain squares or another pieced block. Its design forms an overall pattern or chain across the quilt.

The Puss in a Corner shown in no. 63 is set together without lattice, making a more solid design in the center. The white spaces are quilted with a heart-and-feather design, which forms an arc surrounding the more solid portion of the design. Random shades of blue were used for this scrap quilt, which was pieced in a Template-Free™ method.

Burgoyne Surrounded

Burgoyne Surrounded is the popular name for a design that is nearly identical to a pattern woven into coverlets. Mountain Mist patterns refer to this design as "Homespun." The quilt design supposedly represents the battle plan and formation of soldiers in the American Revolutionary War, when the British under General John Burgoyne were forced to surrender at Saratoga on 17 October 1777. This battle was the turning point of the war. A British quilting book refers to the name as one being from "an incident from the Revolutionary period. In this pattern, the larger red English infantry square is encircled by files of small squares, the American irregulars."[54]

The Burgoyne Surrounded quilt shown in no. 64 was quickly pieced with a Template-Free™ method. Early quilters may have torn strips and used a similar method. Two classic designs are used for the quilting: a grid in the center portion and a cable for the border.

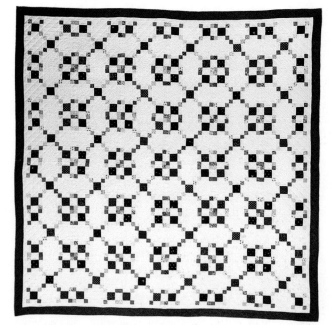

63. Puss in a Corner, 1985, made by Nancy J. Martin, Woodinville, Washington, 80 x 80 inches, pieced cottons. (Collection of That Patchwork Place, Inc.)

64. Burgoyne Surrounded, 1989, made by Nancy J. Martin, Woodinville, Washington, 69 x 85 inches, pieced cottons. (Collection of That Patchwork Place, Inc.)

PATTERNS
FOR MAKING YOUR
OWN QUILTS

65. Chintz Medallion, 1989, made by Nancy J. Martin, Woodinville, Washington, 84 x 84 inches, pieced cottons. (Collection of That Patchwork Place, Inc.)

MAKING A CHINTZ MEDALLION QUILT

In England, medallion quilts were often made from chintz fabric, featuring a particularly interesting piece of chintz or specially printed center panel. Various pieces of chintz were cut into squares and used to surround the center panel. Often, an assortment of chintzes from a sample book was used, making the quilt a showcase of elaborate prints.

In addition to the cotton prints that are reminiscent of the old chintz fabrics, many other interesting chintz prints are available today. This quilt design is an excellent way to highlight your favorite fabric in the center panel and then add coordinating pieces of all those new prints you may have been wanting to purchase.

Leftover home-decorating fabrics can also be utilized in a chintz medallion quilt. These are 100% cotton fabrics normally used for draperies, slipcovers, and pillows. The larger scale of the chintzes and decorator prints creates interest when combined with other fabrics in a quilt. Many have a glazed finish, which adds a shine or light reflectiveness to the quilt's surface. Although these fabrics are heavier than more traditional quilt fabrics, they are not difficult to work with. However, since decorator fabrics may add extra bulk to the seams of your quilt, be sure to plan the quilting design to avoid close quilting in these areas.

Chintz Medallion Quilt

Dimensions: 84″ x 84″

Measurements for borders and pattern pieces include ¼″ seam allowances.

Materials: 45″ wide fabric
¾ yd. each of 8 assorted chintz prints*
½ yd. striped fabric for inner border
1⅜ yds. fabric for outer border (cut on crosswise grain)
      and frame for chintz panel
5 yds. fabric for backing
Batting, binding, and thread to finish

*Scraps of chintz fabric may be substituted in varying amounts.

Directions

1. Cut or cut and frame a piece of fabric for center panel, 17″ x 17″. Finished size of panel will be 16½″ x 16½″.
2. Cut all necessary fabric pieces and organize in a pleasing arrangement.
3. Piece 19 Template #1, 2 Template #2, and 1 Template #3 to form 2 side panel segments.

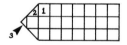

4. Join a side panel segment to opposite sides of the center panel.

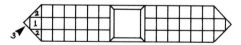

5. Piece the remaining 2 corner segments in rows to form a pyramid shape. Join to center panel.

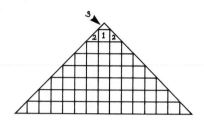

6. Add inner borders to opposite sides, then to top and bottom of quilt top.
      Two strips 2″ x 70½″
      Two strips 2″ x 73½″
7. Add outer borders to opposite sides, then to top and bottom of quilt top:
      Two strips 6″ x 73½″
      Two strips 6″ x 84″
8. Add batting and backing; quilt or tie.
9. Bind with bias strips of fabric.

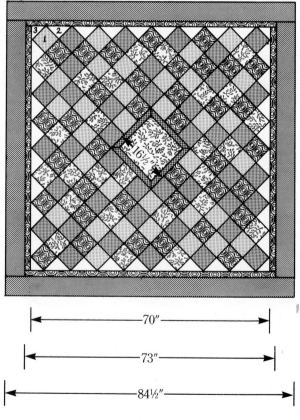

Quilt Plan

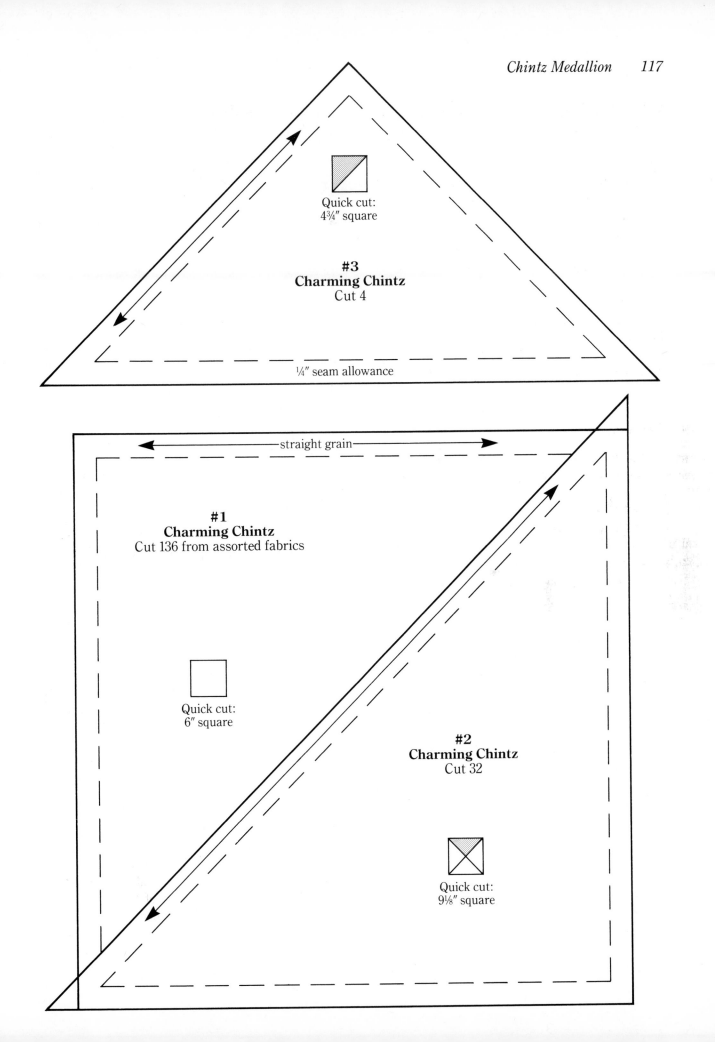

Quick cut:
4¾" square

#3
Charming Chintz
Cut 4

¼" seam allowance

←————— straight grain —————→

#1
Charming Chintz
Cut 136 from assorted fabrics

Quick cut:
6" square

#2
Charming Chintz
Cut 32

Quick cut:
9⅛" square

66. Strippy Stars, 1989, made by
Nancy J. Martin, Woodinville,
Washington, 77½ x 73 inches,
pieced cottons. (Collection of
That Patchwork Place, Inc.)

MAKING A STRIPPY QUILT

Most strippy quilts found in the United States feature pieced blocks set "on point" in vertical rows with strips of fabric separating the rows. Simple blocks, such as Four Patches, Ninepatches, and Variable Stars, were often used. Templates for blocks you may want to use in your strippy quilt are found on pages 122 and 123. Don't hesitate to substitute a different block to your liking. Using the directions below and the Basic Techniques found on pages 168–173, you can create a contemporary version of this old quilt style.

Materials

The needed materials cannot be determined until a quilt plan is devised (Steps 1, 2, 3, 4). It is fun to make the blocks from an existing fabric supply, for the scrap bag was the traditional fabric source for a strippy quilt. New material may be purchased for the setting triangles and joining strips. The 58½" x 62" quilt plan shown on page 120 uses 7" blocks and requires 1½ yards of fabric for the setting triangles and 1½ yards of a figured stripe for the joining strips. Vary your purchase according to the size of your quilt. Striped fabric, especially a figured or floral stripe, is a good choice for the joining strips. Or use a solid color or plain muslin if you wish to highlight your quilting stitches. You need to purchase enough continuous yardage for the joining strips so that each strip can be cut from the lengthwise grain of fabric. If you are using borders and are cutting them from the lengthwise grain of fabric rather than piecing them from crosswise strips, you will also need to purchase continuous yardage of the fabric.

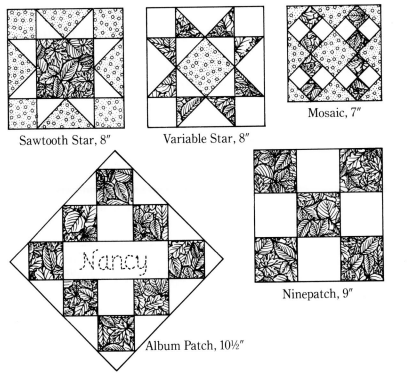

Sawtooth Star, 8″

Variable Star, 8″

Mosaic, 7″

Nancy

Album Patch, 10½″

Ninepatch, 9″

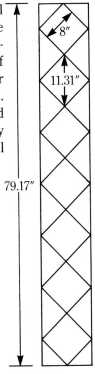

2. Using the diagonal measurements, prepare a quilt plan. First, determine the number of blocks you will need for the length of your quilt. Using an 8″ finished block, seven diagonally set blocks would equal a 79.17″ length.

General Planning

1. Since blocks in a strippy quilt are usually set "on point" (see Album Patch block above), you'll need to know the diagonal measurements of the block. Determine which block you'll be using and multiply the finished block size by 1.414 to find this measurement. Here is a handy chart to use for the most common size blocks:

Size of Block	Diagonal Measurement
6″	8.48
6½″	9.19
7″	9.90
7½″	10.61
8″	11.31
8½″	12.02
9″	12.73
9½″	13.43
10″	14.14
10½″	14.85
11″	15.55
11½″	16.26
12″	16.97

Most sewing measurements are given in inches, so this chart will help you convert from decimals to inches.

1/16 = .06	½ = .5
⅛ = .125	⅝ = .625
¼ = .25	¾ = .78
⅜ = .375	⅞ = .875

3. Next, determine the width by adding joining strips between the vertical rows. Using an 8″ finished block, four vertical rows of blocks joined by three 8″ wide strips of fabric would give you a 69¼″ width.

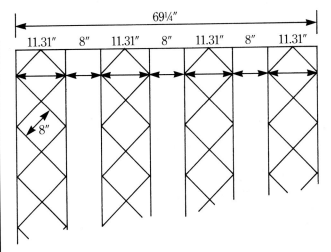

4. Add wide borders to the quilt plan, if desired.

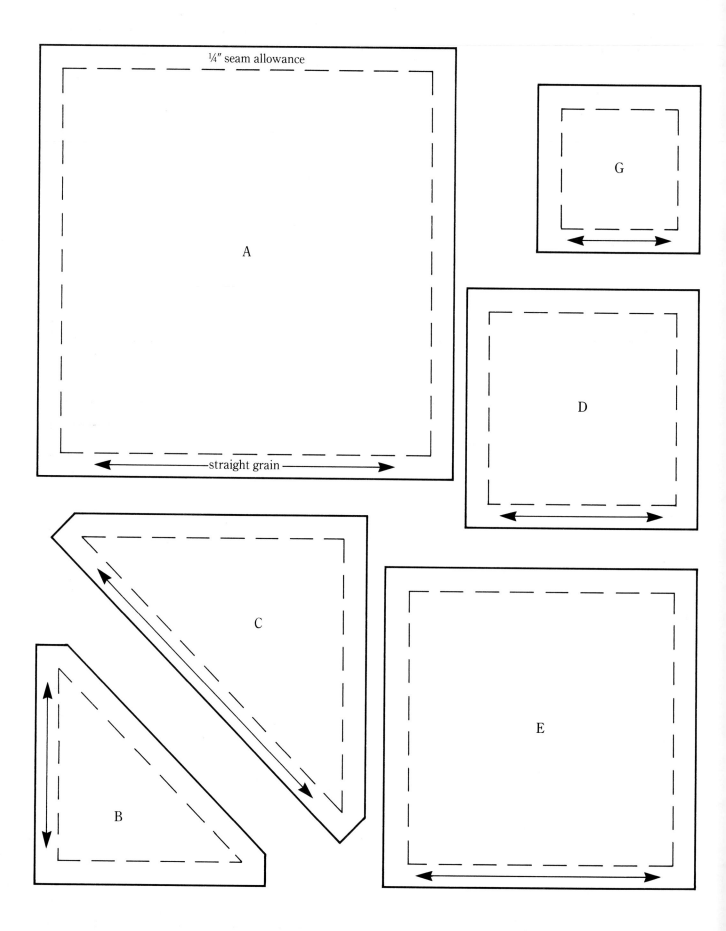

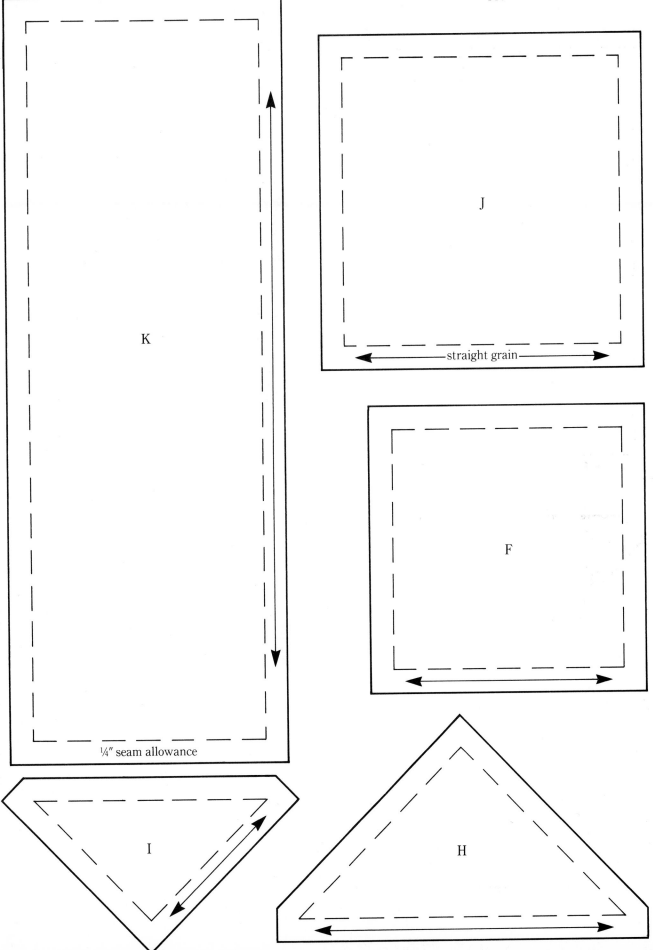

K

J

straight grain

¼" seam allowance

F

I

H

MAKING A SUNSHINE AND SHADOWS QUILT

By arranging the light and dark sides of a block, you can achieve a number of variations of the Sunshine and Shadows design. The most common arrangements of this design are Log Cabin blocks, which have several variations:

Patterns included in this section are for Log Cabin, Courthouse Steps, Pineapple, and Shaded Four-Patch blocks, all of which are set in different dark and light arrangements. These blocks are set together without lattice to form an overall design. Construct the number of blocks needed to achieve the finished size. Borders may be added, if desired.

Barn Raising

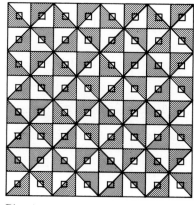

Pinwheel

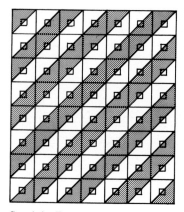

Straight Furrows

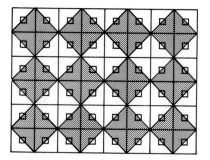

Sunshine and Shadows

Zig Zag

The patterns are graded as to difficulty:

Beginner

Intermediate

Advanced

Use this information to help you select a project in keeping with your skills. To make templates from these patterns, see page 142.

The easiest Sunshine and Shadows block to experiment with is the Shaded Four-Patch pattern found on page 130. Quick and easy to piece, it can be effectively used in any of the settings shown here. The pattern is based on an antique top made by Clara Countryman in Wyoming, Iowa, about 1920 (no. 45). Select scraps of fabrics including plaids, checks, dots, and homespun to achieve the mellow look of an "older" quilt. Contemporary versions of this quilt are shown here.

67. Sunshine and Shadows, 1986,
made by Nancy J. Martin,
Woodinville, Washington, 52 x 60
inches, pieced cottons. (Collection
of That Patchwork Place, Inc.)

68. Sunshine and Shadows, 1989,
made by Suzanne Hammond,
Bellingham, Washington,
38 x 46 inches, pieced cottons.
(Collection of the artist)

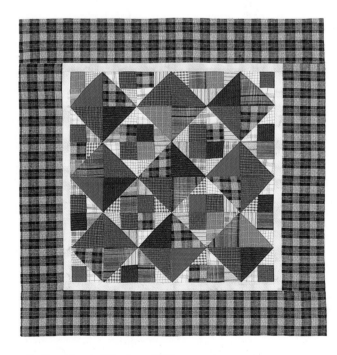

69. Sunshine and Shadows, 1989,
made by Suzanne Hammond,
Bellingham, Washington, 35 x 35
inches, pieced cottons.
(Collection of the artist)

70. Sunshine and Shadows, 1989,
made by Nancy J. Martin,
Woodinville, Washington, 44 x 52
inches, pieced cottons. (Collection
of That Patchwork Place, Inc.)

LOG CABIN

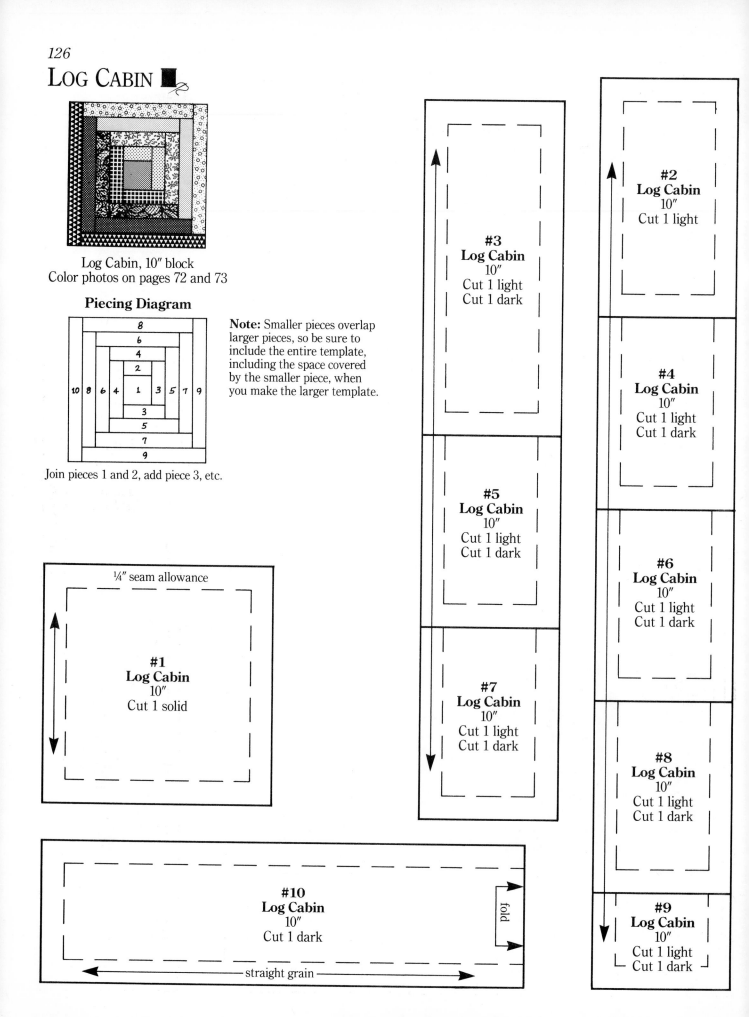

Log Cabin, 10″ block
Color photos on pages 72 and 73

Piecing Diagram

		8		
		6		
		4		
		2		
10 8 6 4		1	3 5 7 9	
		3		
		5		
		7		
		9		

Join pieces 1 and 2, add piece 3, etc.

Note: Smaller pieces overlap larger pieces, so be sure to include the entire template, including the space covered by the smaller piece, when you make the larger template.

¼″ seam allowance

#1
Log Cabin
10″
Cut 1 solid

#10
Log Cabin
10″
Cut 1 dark

fold

straight grain

#3
Log Cabin
10″
Cut 1 light
Cut 1 dark

#5
Log Cabin
10″
Cut 1 light
Cut 1 dark

#7
Log Cabin
10″
Cut 1 light
Cut 1 dark

#2
Log Cabin
10″
Cut 1 light

#4
Log Cabin
10″
Cut 1 light
Cut 1 dark

#6
Log Cabin
10″
Cut 1 light
Cut 1 dark

#8
Log Cabin
10″
Cut 1 light
Cut 1 dark

#9
Log Cabin
10″
Cut 1 light
Cut 1 dark

COURTHOUSE STEPS

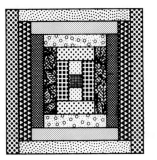

Courthouse Steps, 11″ block
Color photos on pages 74, 75, and 77

Piecing Diagram

					5						
					4						
					3						
				2						
				1						
6	5	4	3	2	1 1	2	3	4	5	6
					1						
					2						
					3						
					4						
					5						

Note: Smaller pieces overlap larger pieces, so be sure to include the entire template, including the space covered by the smaller piece, when you make the larger template.

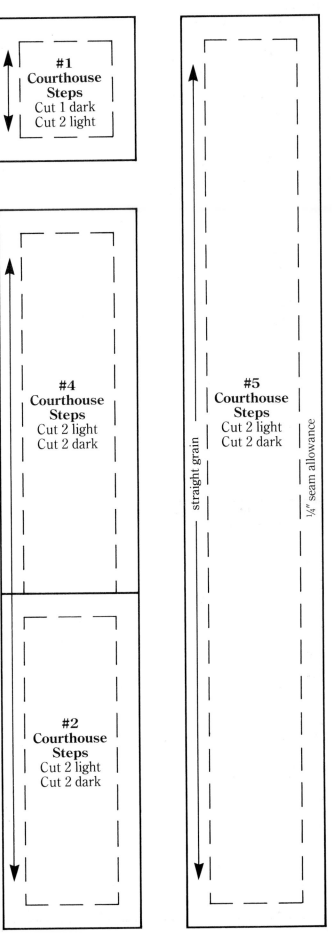

#1 Courthouse Steps
Cut 1 dark
Cut 2 light

#4 Courthouse Steps
Cut 2 light
Cut 2 dark

#5 Courthouse Steps
Cut 2 light
Cut 2 dark

straight grain

¼″ seam allowance

#2 Courthouse Steps
Cut 2 light
Cut 2 dark

#6 Courthouse Steps
Cut 2 dark

Place on fold

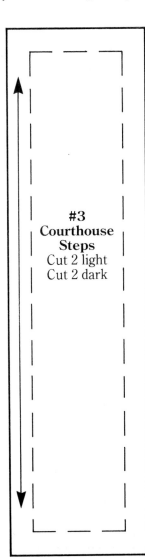

#3 Courthouse Steps
Cut 2 light
Cut 2 dark

PINEAPPLE

©Marsha McCloskey, 1983

Pineapple, 12″ block
Color photos on pages 78 and 79

Piecing Diagram

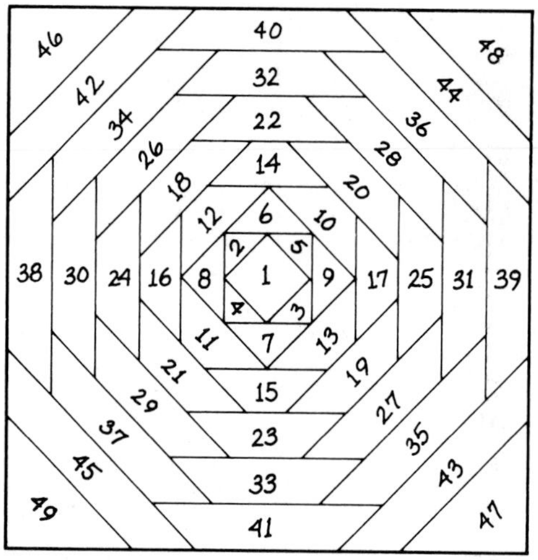

Note: Numbers refer to the order in which templates are added to the center, *not* the piecing sequence.

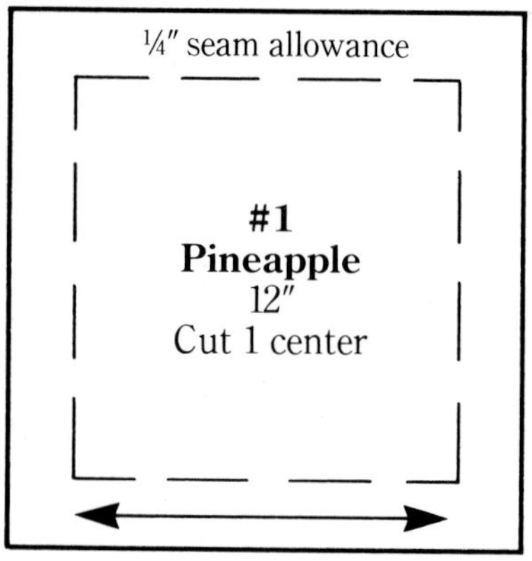

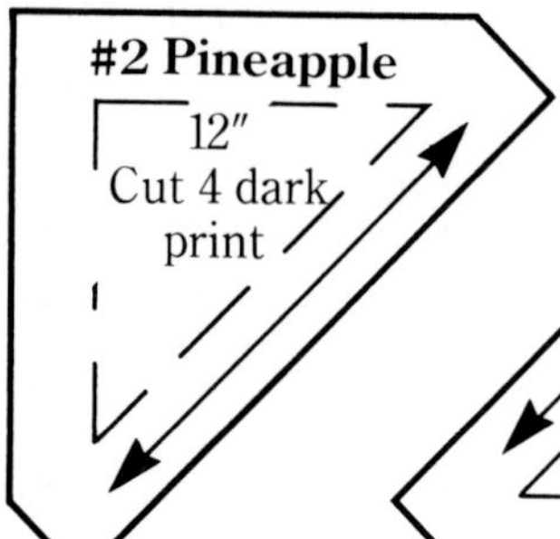

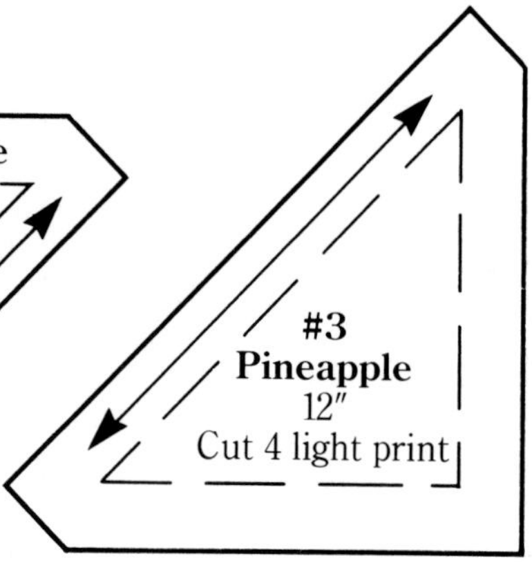

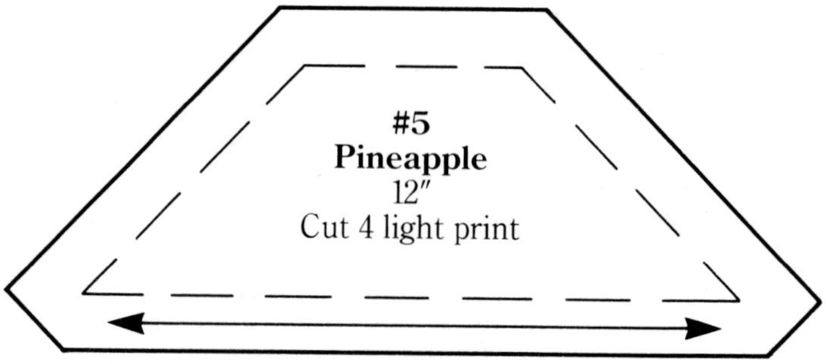

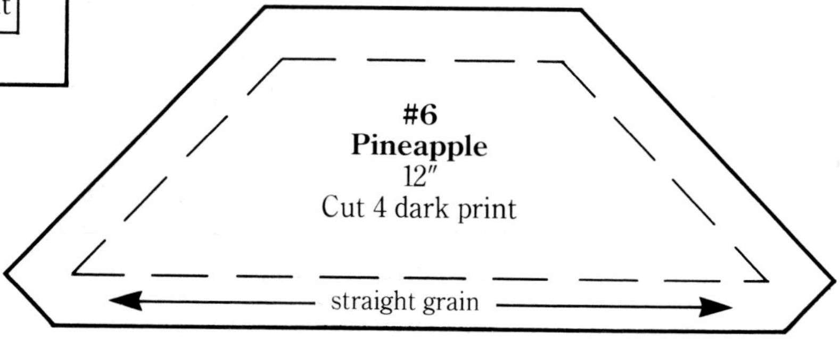

¼″ seam allowance

**#1
Pineapple
12″
Cut 1 center**

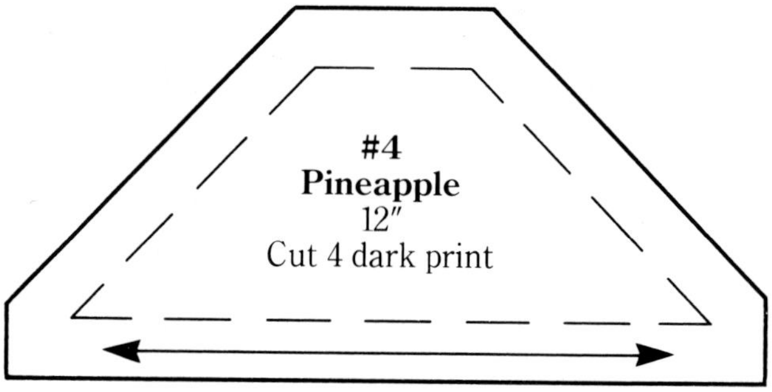

**#4
Pineapple
12″
Cut 4 dark print**

**#2 Pineapple
12″
Cut 4 dark print**

**#3
Pineapple
12″
Cut 4 light print**

**#5
Pineapple
12″
Cut 4 light print**

**#6
Pineapple
12″
Cut 4 dark print**

straight grain

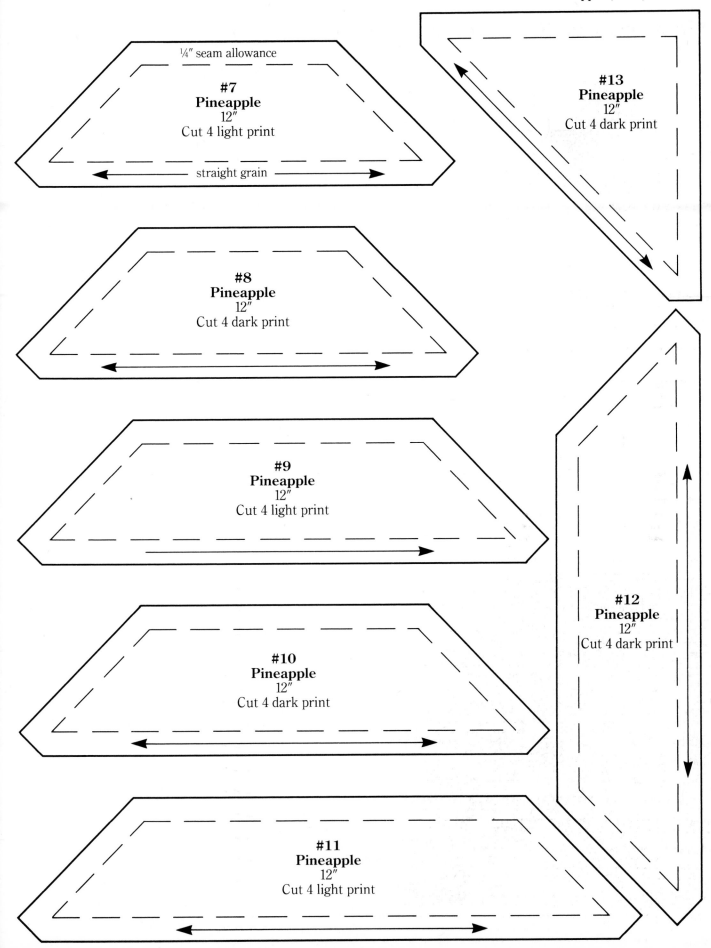

¼″ seam allowance

#7
Pineapple
12″
Cut 4 light print

straight grain

#13
Pineapple
12″
Cut 4 dark print

#8
Pineapple
12″
Cut 4 dark print

#9
Pineapple
12″
Cut 4 light print

#12
Pineapple
12″
Cut 4 dark print

#10
Pineapple
12″
Cut 4 dark print

#11
Pineapple
12″
Cut 4 light print

SHADED FOUR PATCH ▪

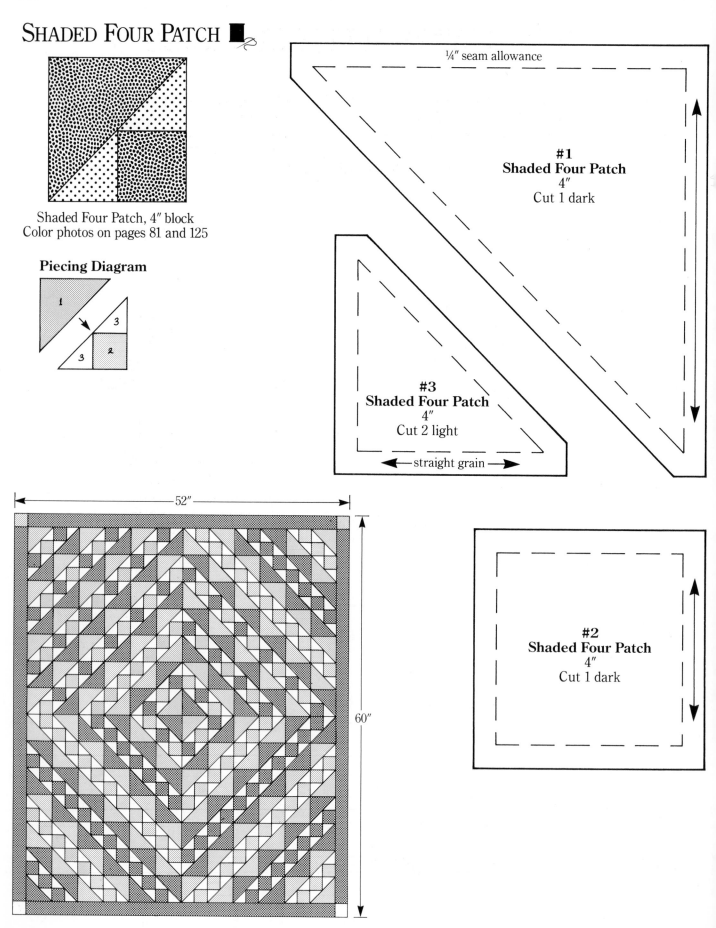

Shaded Four Patch, 4″ block
Color photos on pages 81 and 125

Piecing Diagram

¼″ seam allowance

**#1
Shaded Four Patch**
4″
Cut 1 dark

**#3
Shaded Four Patch**
4″
Cut 2 light

← straight grain →

**#2
Shaded Four Patch**
4″
Cut 1 dark

52″

60″

QUICK WAYS WITH CLASSICS

Timesaving Template-Free™ methods eliminate much of the tedium associated with making classic quilts. Using a sewing machine, rotary cutter and mat, and Bias Square™, you can quickly create these classics. All of the quilts in this section are constructed from strips of fabric cut with a rotary cutter.

Burgoyne Surrounded and Puss in a Corner use strip piecing, where crosswise strips are sewn into segments and then cut into units. More information on these quiltmaking techniques can be found in this section.

The Oak Leaf Medallion with Sawtooth Borders and the Tree of Life quilts use bias squares in their construction. Bias squares are squares consisting of a light and a dark triangle, which have been cut from pieced bias strips of fabric. See page 133 for more details on this method.

Strip Piecing

Rather than cutting out pieces individually, many quiltmakers feel that strip piecing is a faster way to work. Long fabric strips are sewn together in units called segments and then subcut into shorter portions; the small units are then recombined to form simple designs. Strip piecing is a great time-saver when you are working with squares and rectangles that will be combined in identical colors and in repeated units.

To determine the width to cut strips, add a ¼" seam allowance to each side of the finished dimension on the desired shape. For example, if the finished dimension of a square will be 2", cut 2½" strips. For the quilts given here, cutting dimensions for squares and rectangles are provided in the directions.

Cut strips from the crosswise grain of the fabric. Fold the fabric so two or four layers can be cut at one time. Mark strip widths and cut with sharp scissors or use a rotary cutter and ruler. Take care and be accurate. Time saved with quick methods is wasted if the work is done poorly.

Sew long strips together with ¼" seam allowances. Press seam allowances toward the darker fabric, pressing from the front of the work so the fabric won't pleat along the seam lines. Usually, pressing toward the dark will result in opposing seams at points of matching. If the coloring of the strips doesn't work out that way, press for opposing seams instead of always to the dark.

For subcuts, measure and mark crosswise cuts, using templates or rotary cutter and ruler. Join strip-pieced units, as shown in the illustrations, to make Four-Patch, Ninepatch, and other desired units.

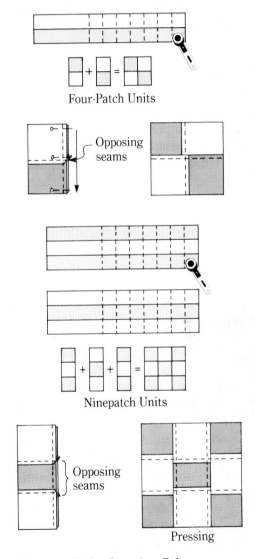

Four-Patch Units

Opposing seams

Ninepatch Units

Opposing seams

Pressing

Working with Grain Lines

Thread is woven together to form fabric. It stretches or remains stable, depending on the grain line that you are using. Lengthwise grain runs parallel to the selvage and has very little stretch. Crosswise grain runs from selvage to selvage and has some "give" to it. All other grains are considered bias. True

BURGOYNE SURROUNDED

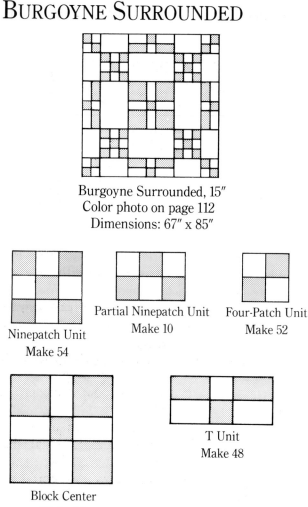

Burgoyne Surrounded, 15″
Color photo on page 112
Dimensions: 67″ x 85″

Ninepatch Unit
Make 54

Partial Ninepatch Unit
Make 10

Four-Patch Unit
Make 52

T Unit
Make 48

Block Center
Make 12

Materials: 45″ wide fabric

5¼ yds. muslin for background and borders
1¾ yds. dark fabric for blocks
4 yds. fabric for backing
Batting, binding, and thread to finish

Cutting and Subcutting:

All strips are cut crosswise from selvage to selvage.

1. Cut muslin for borders as follows:
    Two strips 6½″ x 73½″ for sides
    Two strips 6½″ x 67″ for top and bottom
2. For Ninepatch and partial Ninepatch units, cut 11 strips 1½″ wide from background fabric and 13 strips 1½″ wide from dark fabric. Stitch strips together to make 5 sets of strips for Segment I and 3 sets of strips for Segment II.

Subcut these rows of strips 1½″ wide so that you have 118 Segment I units and 64 Segment II units.

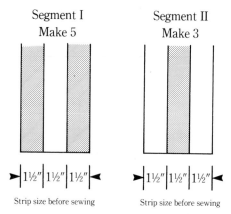

Segment I
Make 5

Segment II
Make 3

Strip size before sewing

Strip size before sewing

3. For Four-Patch units, cut 4 strips 1½″ wide from background fabric and 4 strips 1½″ wide from dark fabric. Stitch strips to make 4 sets of strips.

    Subcut into 1½″ segments so that you have 104 segments to join into Four Patches.

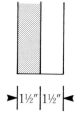

Strip size before sewing

4. For T Units, cut 2 strips 1½″ wide from background fabric and 4 strips 2½″ wide from dark fabric. Stitch strips together to form 2 sets of strips for Segment I. Cut 4 strips 2½″ wide from background fabric and 2 strips 1½″ wide from dark fabric. Stitch strips together to form 2 sets of strips for Segment II.

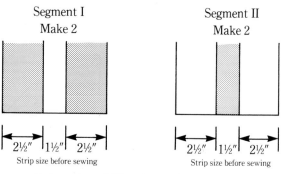

Segment I
Make 2

Segment II
Make 2

Strip size before sewing

Strip size before sewing

Subcut into 1½″ units so that you have 48 each from segments I and II to join into T units.

5. For block centers, cut 4 strips 2½″ wide from dark fabric and 2 strips 1½″ wide from background fab-

ric. Stitch strips together to form 2 sets of strips for Segment I. Cut 2 strips 2½″ wide from background fabric and 1 strip 1½″ wide from dark fabric. Stitch strips together to make Segment II.

Segment I
Make 2

Segment II
Make 1

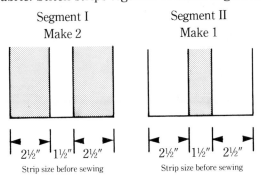

Subcut Segment I into 2½″ wide units so that you have 24 to join into block centers. Subcut Segment II into 1½″ wide units so that you have 12 to join into block centers.

6. Cut 48 rectangles 3½″ x 5½″ and 96 rectangles 2½″ x 3½″ from background fabric.
7. Cut 17 lattice strips 3½″ x 15½″ and 14 lattice strips 2½″ x 15½″ from background fabric.

Directions

1. Piece 54 Ninepatch units, 10 partial Ninepatch units, 52 Four-Patch units, 12 block centers, and 48 T units.

2. Assemble into 12 Burgoyne Surrounded blocks.

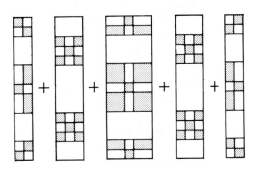

3. Stitch 3 blocks and 2 lattice strips, 3½″ wide, into a row. Add a 2½″ wide lattice strip to the end of each row. Make 4 rows.
4. Stitch 2 rows of lattice for top and bottom of quilt from 2 Four Patches, 2 partial Ninepatches, and 2½″ wide lattice strips.
5. Make 3 rows of lattice from 2 Ninepatches, 2 partial Ninepatches, and 3 lattice strips.
6. Assemble quilt top, alternating rows of blocks and lattice strips, as shown below.
7. Add border strips, stitching blunt-sewn corners.
8. Add batting and backing; quilt or tie. Quilting suggestion: Quilt a grid in center portion of quilt and use a traditional cable design in the border.
9. Bind with bias strips.

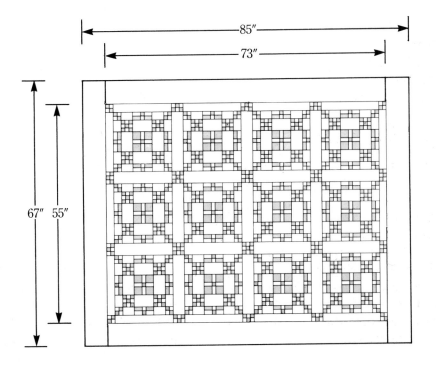

PUSS IN THE CORNER

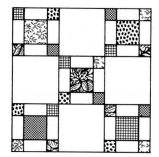

Puss in the Corner, 12″ block
Color photo on page 112
Dimensions: 80″ x 80″

Measurements for borders and pattern pieces include ¼″ seam allowance.

Materials: 45″ wide fabric

4½ yds. light background fabric for blocks and inner border
3 yds. assorted blue fabrics (allow ⅞ yd. of single fabric for border)
4⅝ yds. fabric for backing
Batting, binding, and thread to finish

Cutting

All measurements include ¼″ seam allowance. Do not add to the sizes given.

1. Cut 144 squares 4½″ x 4½″ from light fabric.
2. Cut 12 strips 2½″ wide from assorted blue fabrics for Segment I.
3. Cut 24 strips 1½″ wide from light fabric for Segment I.
4. Cut 14 strips 2½″ wide from light fabric for Segment II.
5. Cut 28 strips 1½″ wide from assorted blue fabrics for Segment II.

Puss-in-the-Corner Units

1. Stitch strips together to make 12 sets of strips for Segment I, which looks like this:

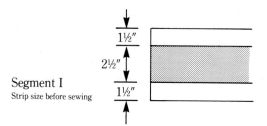

Segment I
Strip size before sewing

2. Subcut Segment I into 180 units, each 2½″.
3. Stitch strips together to make 14 sets of strips for Segment II, which looks like this:

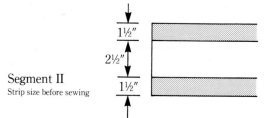

Segment II
Strip size before sewing

4. Subcut Segment II into 360 units, each 1½″.
5. Assemble a unit from Segment I between 2 units from Segment II for each Puss-in-the-Corner unit.

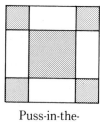

Puss-in-the-
Corner unit

Directions for Quilt Assembly

1. Using four 4½″ light squares and 5 Puss-in-the-Corner units, assemble a 12½″ Puss-in-the-Corner block according to diagram. Repeat to make 36 blocks.

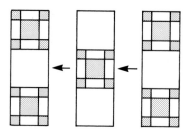

2. Set together in rows, as shown in diagram on next page.
3. Using diagram and measurements on the following page, cut inner border strips 1½″ wide from light fabric and outer border strips 3½″ wide from blue fabric. Borders are pieced from crosswise-cut strips. Stitch to quilt, using mitered or blunt-sewn corners and adjusting to fit.
4. Add batting and backing; quilt. Quilting suggestion: Use a heart and feather design that forms an arc around the more solid center section.
5. Bind with bias strip of fabric.

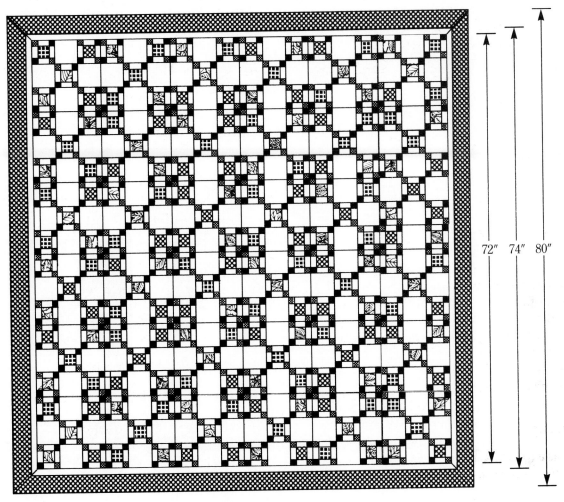

Quilt Plan

TREE OF LIFE

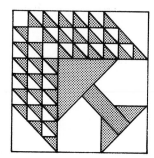

Tree of Life, 18″ block
Color photo on page 111
Dimensions: 72″ x 90″

Materials: 45″ wide fabric
5 yds. muslin or light background fabric
3 yds. red fabric
3 yds. green fabric
5¼ yds. fabric for backing
Batting, binding, and thread to finish

Templates

Templates are given only for pattern pieces 2 and 6. The remaining pattern pieces are rotary cut. The pattern piece number in the directions refers to their placement on the Piecing Diagram.

Cutting

All measurements include ¼″ seam allowance. Do not add seam allowance to the sizes given.

1. Cut 2½″ wide strips from red, green, and light fabrics. Use bias square directions found on page 133 to make 360 bias square units 2½″ x 2½″ in the red-and-light combination and 240 bias square units 2½″ x 2½″ in the green-and-light combination.
2. Utilizing Template #2 and waste triangles, cut 120 triangles from red fabric.
3. Cut 60 squares 2½″ x 2½″ from light fabric (Template #1).
4. Cut 10 squares 8⅞″ x 8⅞″ from green fabric. Cut once diagonally (Template #3).
5. Cut 30 squares 6⅞″ x 6⅞″ from light fabric. Cut once diagonally (Template #4).
6. Cut 20 rectangles 2½″ x 7¼″ from green fabric (Template #5).
7. Using Template #6, cut 20 and 20 R from light fabric.
8. Cut 20 squares 4⅛″ x 4⅛″ from green fabric. Cut once diagonally (Template #7).

Directions

1. Cut and piece 20 Tree of Life blocks.

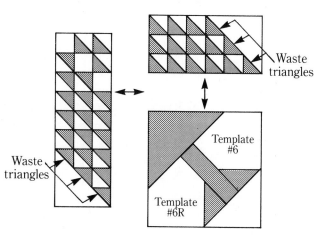

2. Set together in rows, as shown below.

3. Add batting and backing; quilt or tie. Quilting suggestion: Quilt ¼″ away from small triangle pieces. Quilt decreasing smaller triangles inside the large triangular pieces of background and tree trunk. Quilt a cross-hatch grid in remaining background fabric on either side of tree trunk.
4. Bind with bias strips of fabric.

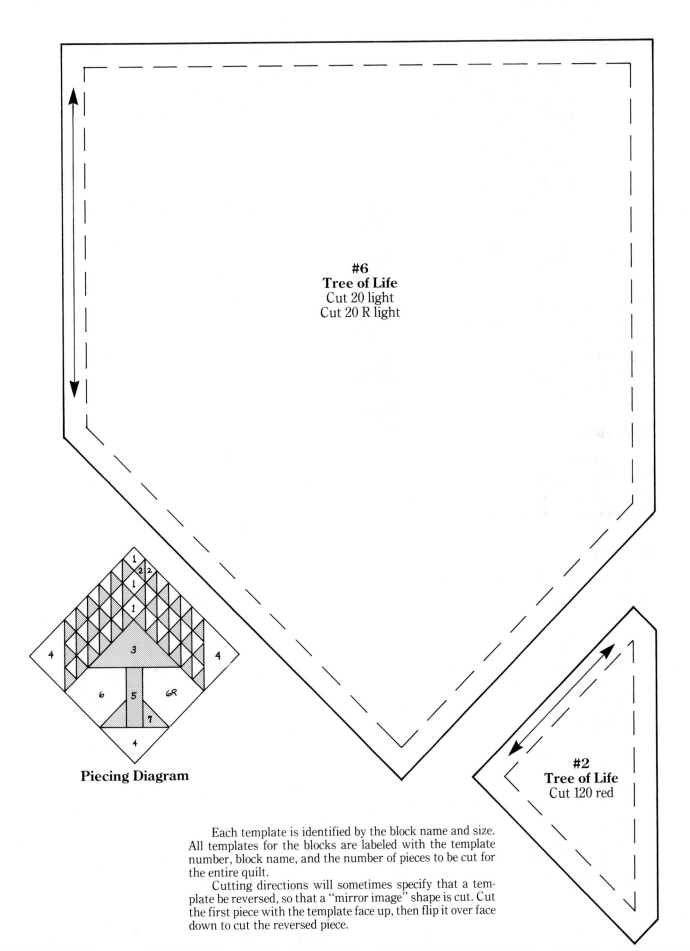

#6
Tree of Life
Cut 20 light
Cut 20 R light

Piecing Diagram

#2
Tree of Life
Cut 120 red

Each template is identified by the block name and size. All templates for the blocks are labeled with the template number, block name, and the number of pieces to be cut for the entire quilt.

Cutting directions will sometimes specify that a template be reversed, so that a "mirror image" shape is cut. Cut the first piece with the template face up, then flip it over face down to cut the reversed piece.

OAK LEAF MEDALLION WITH SAWTOOTH BORDERS

Color photo on page 110
Dimensions: 75″ x 75″

Materials: 45″ wide fabric
3 yds. muslin or light background fabric
3 yds. navy print fabric
4½ yds. fabric for backing
Batting, binding, and thread to finish

Cutting

All measurements include ¼″ seam allowance. Do not add seam allowances to the sizes given.

1. Cut 3½″ wide strips from light and navy fabrics. Use bias square directions found on page 133 to make 144 bias square units 3½″ x 3½″. From this same fabric, cut 12 bias squares 3⁵⁄₁₆″ x 3⁵⁄₁₆″ for corner units.
2. Cut center square 21½″ x 21½″ from light fabric.
3. Cut 4 strips 6½″ x 27½″ from navy fabric for first border.
4. Cut 2 squares 6⅞″ x 6⅞″ from navy fabric. Cut once diagonally for 4 first border inner corners.
5. Cut 2 squares 8⅞″ x 8⅞″ from navy fabric. Cut once diagonally for 4 first border outer corners.
6. From light fabric, cut 2 strips 6½″ x 45½″ and 2 strips 6½″ x 57½″ for middle border.
7. From navy fabric, cut 2 strips 6½″ x 63½″ and 2 strips 6½″ x 75½″ for outer border.
8. Cut 2 squares 2½″ x 2½″ from light fabric and 2 squares 2½″ x 2½″ from navy fabric.
9. Cut Template #1 from navy and light fabrics as directed on pattern piece. Use in corner units.
10. Cut templates for Oak Leaf and Reel appliqué, using templates found on page 164.

Directions

1. Appliqué Oak Leaf and Reel pattern found on page 164 to center of 21½″ x 21½″ piece of light fabric, matching center folds and diagonal creases. To make a quilt similar to the antique quilt shown on page 110, omit templates #2, #4, and #5.
2. Add 7 bias squares 3½″ x 3½″ to both top and bottom of appliqué block, arranging light sides of bias squares next to light sides of block, as shown in quilt plan.
3. Add 9 bias squares 3½″ x 3½″ to each side of appliqué block, arranging light sides as shown in quilt plan.
4. Add a strip of 9 bias squares to one long edge of the four 6½″ x 27½″ navy strips.
5. Add 2 navy strips, 6½″ x 27½″, with bias squares to top and bottom of previous piecing.
6. Construct 4 corner units from 3⁵⁄₁₆″ x 3⁵⁄₁₆″ bias squares, both sizes of navy triangles, and Template #1.

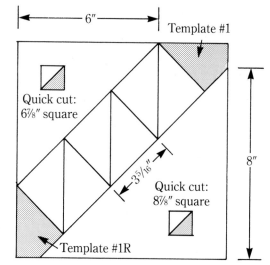

7. Add a 6½″ x 45½″ light fabric strip to top and bottom of quilt.
8. Stitch 6½″ x 57½″ light fabric strips to each side of quilt.
9. Stitch 4 bias square segments of 19 units each, consulting quilt plan for color placement.
10. Stitch a segment to top and bottom of quilt.
11. Add a 2½″ x 2½″ light square and a 2½″ x 2½″ dark square to opposite ends of remaining segments. Using quilt plan as a guide to placement, stitch a segment to each side of quilt.
12. Stitch 6½″ x 63½″ strips to top and bottom of quilt.
13. Add 6½″ x 75½″ borders to sides of quilt.
14. Add batting and backing; quilt or tie. Quilting suggestion: Outline quilt appliqué in center medallion. Quilt a hanging-diamonds grid in the remainder of the quilt.
15. Bind with bias strips of fabric.

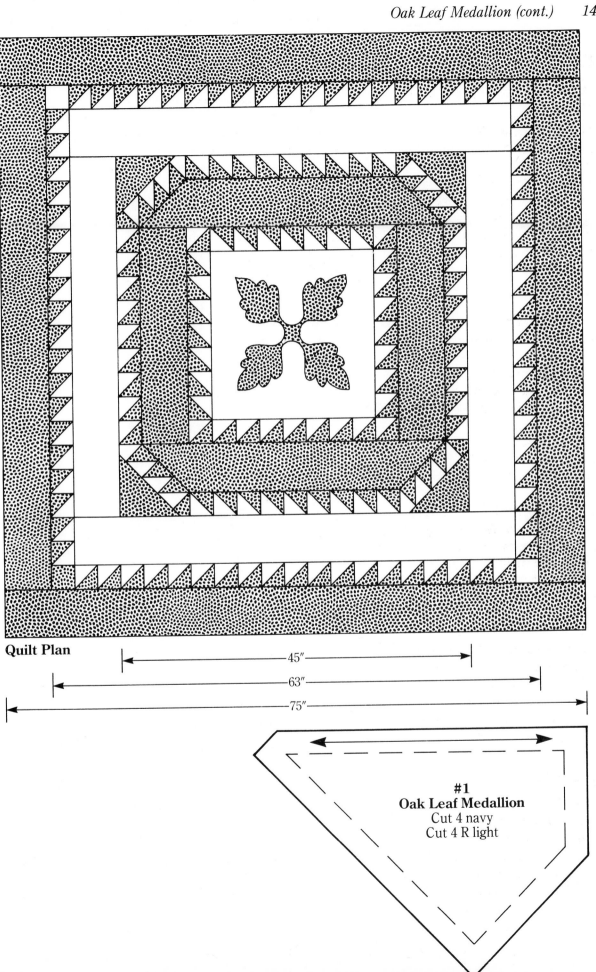

Quilt Plan

|←——————————— 45" ———————————→|
|←————————————— 63" —————————————→|
|←——————————————— 75" ———————————————→|

#1
Oak Leaf Medallion
Cut 4 navy
Cut 4 R light

PATCHWORK AND APPLIQUÉ BLOCKS

In this section, you will find twenty patterns for patchwork and appliqué blocks, which may be used in a variety of ways. A diagram is given for each block, along with its finished size. Ten of the pieced blocks are 12″ square, so they can be adapted into other 12″ block settings. Or, one of each of these 12″ blocks can be incorporated into a sampler quilt. A small quilt plan and color photo reference are provided with most of the pieced blocks. Usually, these refer to the quilt pictured in the color photos. However, in some cases, the setting design used for these antique quilts was too individual or irregular for a quilt, or the blocks were part of the sampler quilt rather than an individual quilt. The finished measurements of the borders and the quilt's outer dimensions are given in each quilt plan. Use these measurements to cut your borders.

The patterns are graded as to difficulty:

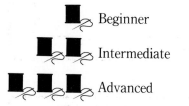

Beginner

Intermediate

Advanced

Use this information to help you select a project in keeping with your skills. Patterns for appliqué blocks are also included. All of these appliqué patterns are 14″ square.

Templates

To make each block, you will need a set of pattern pieces or templates. Carefully trace the templates from the book onto graph paper or tracing paper. Trace accurately and transfer to the paper all information printed on the templates.

Each template for the unit blocks is labeled with a number, the design name, the finished block size, and the number to cut for one block. An "R" in a cutting notation means "reverse." These pieces are mirror images: A notation such as "Cut 2 light, Cut 2 R dark" indicates you cut the first number of pieces with the template face up, then flip it over face down to cut the reverse pieces.

Templates have seam lines (broken lines) as well as cutting lines (solid lines). Grain lines are for the lengthwise or crosswise grain and are shown with an arrow on each piece. Fold lines indicate where half templates are given due to space limitations. Complete the other half of the pattern when you make larger templates. In some cases, smaller pieces overlap larger pieces, so be sure to include the entire template, including the space covered by the smaller piece, when you make the larger templates. Consult the Basic Techniques on pages 168–173 for complete directions on quiltmaking techniques.

ANVIL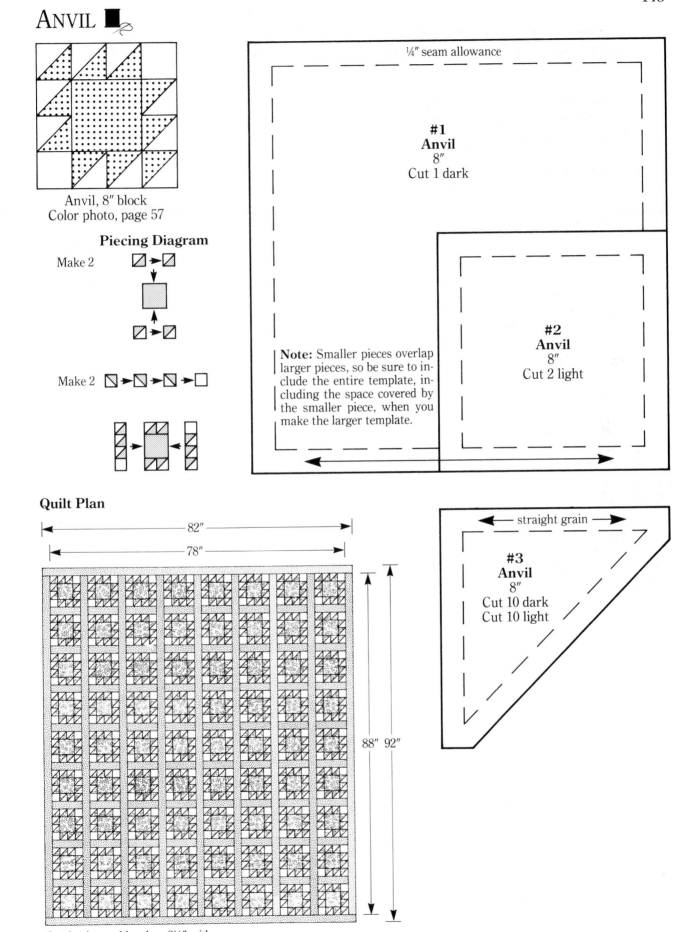

Anvil, 8″ block
Color photo, page 57

Piecing Diagram

Make 2

Make 2

Quilt Plan

Cut lattice and borders 2½″ wide

¼″ seam allowance

#1
Anvil
8″
Cut 1 dark

#2
Anvil
8″
Cut 2 light

Note: Smaller pieces overlap larger pieces, so be sure to include the entire template, including the space covered by the smaller piece, when you make the larger template.

straight grain

#3
Anvil
8″
Cut 10 dark
Cut 10 light

82″

78″

88″ 92″

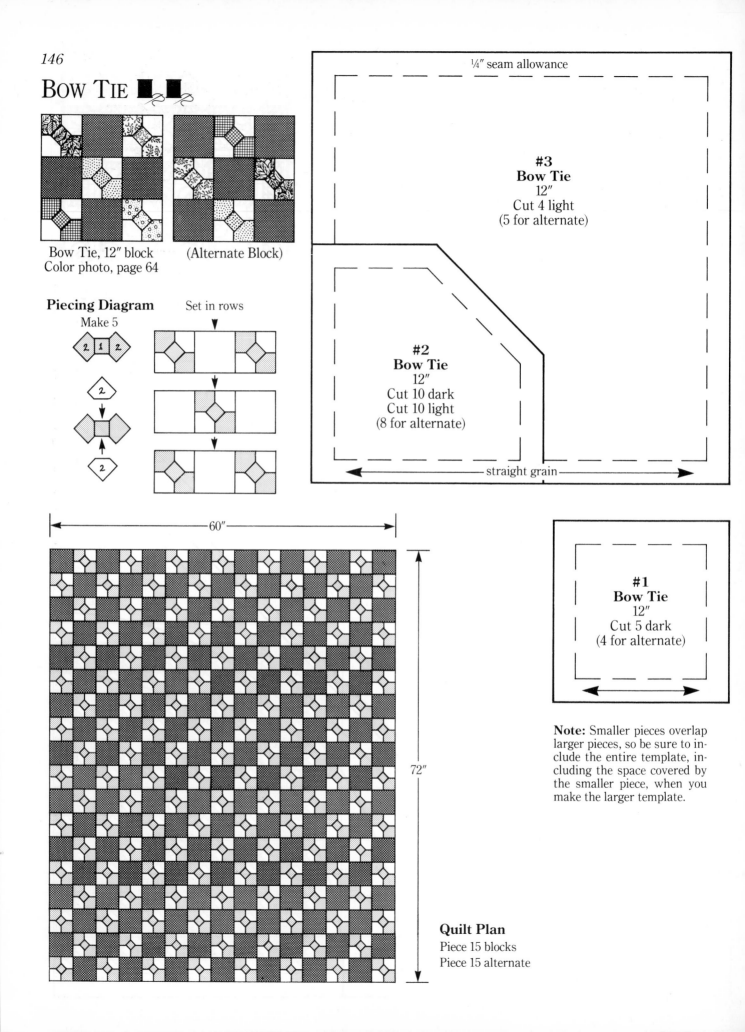

146

BOW TIE

Bow Tie, 12″ block
Color photo, page 64

(Alternate Block)

Piecing Diagram

Make 5

Set in rows

¼″ seam allowance

#3
Bow Tie
12″
Cut 4 light
(5 for alternate)

#2
Bow Tie
12″
Cut 10 dark
Cut 10 light
(8 for alternate)

straight grain

60″

72″

#1
Bow Tie
12″
Cut 5 dark
(4 for alternate)

Note: Smaller pieces overlap larger pieces, so be sure to include the entire template, including the space covered by the smaller piece, when you make the larger template.

Quilt Plan
Piece 15 blocks
Piece 15 alternate

CACTUS BASKET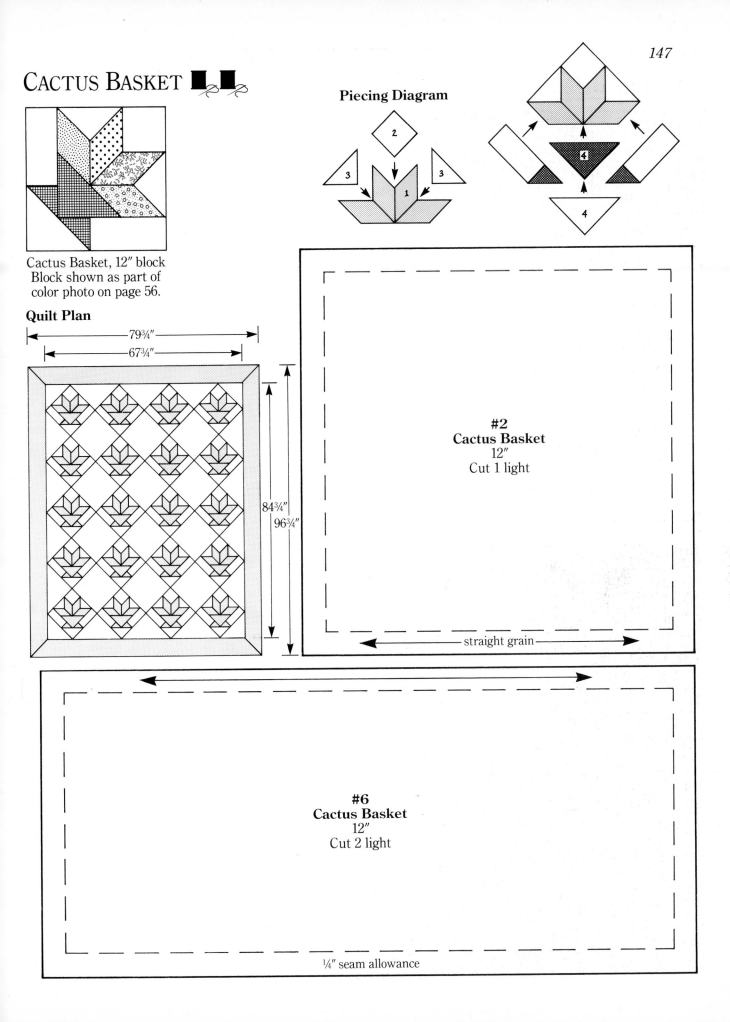

Piecing Diagram

Cactus Basket, 12″ block
Block shown as part of
color photo on page 56.

Quilt Plan

79¾″

67¾″

84¾″
96¾″

#2
Cactus Basket
12″
Cut 1 light

straight grain

#6
Cactus Basket
12″
Cut 2 light

¼″ seam allowance

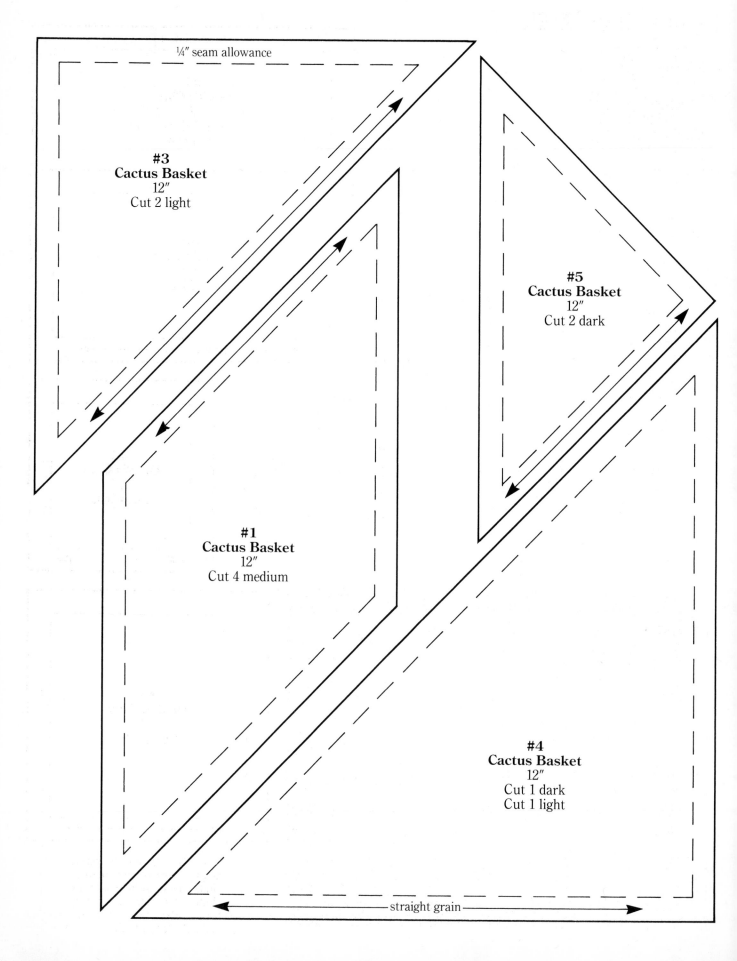

¼" seam allowance

#3
Cactus Basket
12"
Cut 2 light

#5
Cactus Basket
12"
Cut 2 dark

#1
Cactus Basket
12"
Cut 4 medium

#4
Cactus Basket
12"
Cut 1 dark
Cut 1 light

straight grain

DEVIL'S CLAW

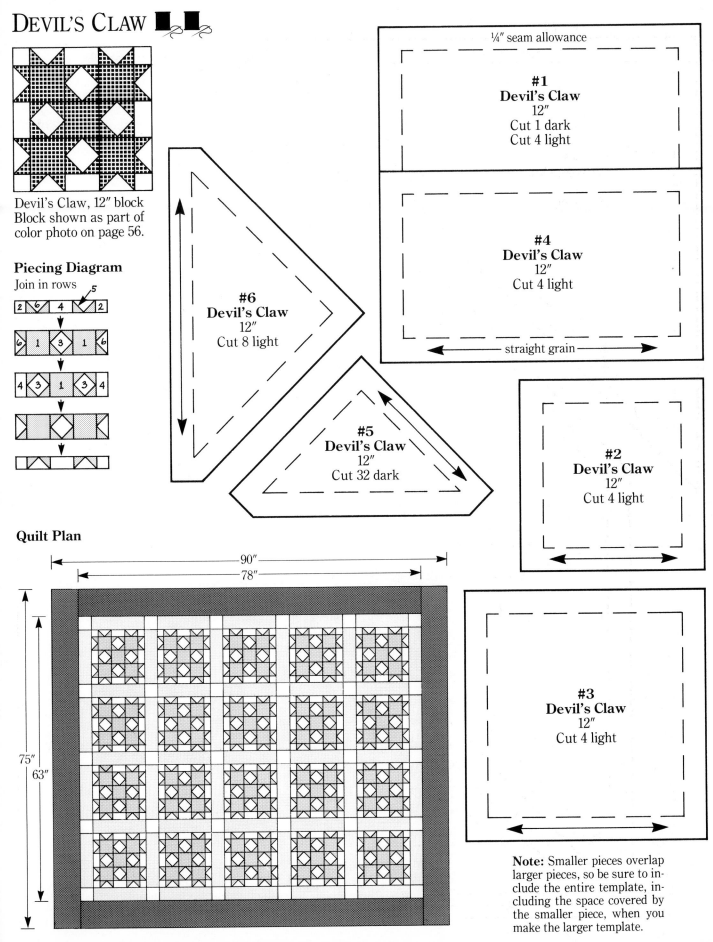

Devil's Claw, 12″ block
Block shown as part of
color photo on page 56.

Piecing Diagram
Join in rows

¼″ seam allowance

#1
Devil's Claw
12″
Cut 1 dark
Cut 4 light

#4
Devil's Claw
12″
Cut 4 light

← straight grain →

#6
Devil's Claw
12″
Cut 8 light

#5
Devil's Claw
12″
Cut 32 dark

#2
Devil's Claw
12″
Cut 4 light

Quilt Plan

90″
78″
75″
63″

#3
Devil's Claw
12″
Cut 4 light

Note: Smaller pieces overlap larger pieces, so be sure to include the entire template, including the space covered by the smaller piece, when you make the larger template.

DOUBLE T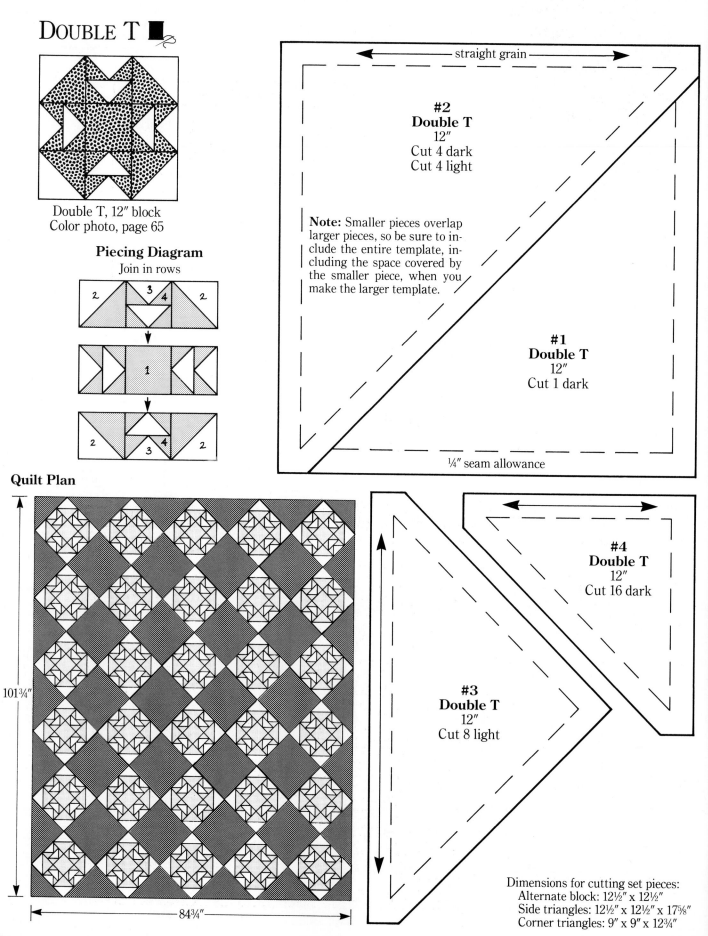

Double T, 12″ block
Color photo, page 65

Piecing Diagram
Join in rows

#2 Double T
12″
Cut 4 dark
Cut 4 light

Note: Smaller pieces overlap larger pieces, so be sure to include the entire template, including the space covered by the smaller piece, when you make the larger template.

straight grain

#1 Double T
12″
Cut 1 dark

¼″ seam allowance

#4 Double T
12″
Cut 16 dark

#3 Double T
12″
Cut 8 light

Quilt Plan

101¾″

84¾″

Dimensions for cutting set pieces:
Alternate block: 12½″ x 12½″
Side triangles: 12½″ x 12½″ x 17⅝″
Corner triangles: 9″ x 9″ x 12¾″

ENVELOPE

Envelope, 12″ block
Block shown as part of
color photo on page 56.

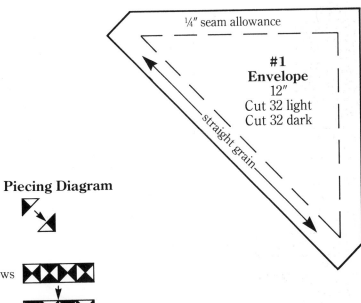

¼″ seam allowance

**#1
Envelope**
12″
Cut 32 light
Cut 32 dark

straight grain

Piecing Diagram

Make 16

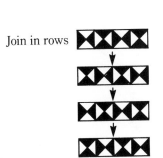

Join in rows

Quilt Plan

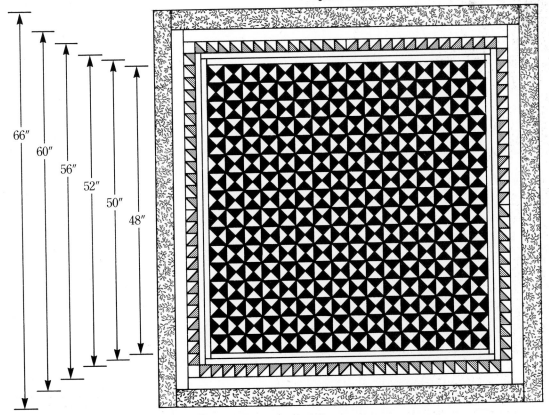

66″

60″

56″

52″

50″

48″

FEATHERED WORLD WITHOUT END ▪▪▪ ©Marsha McCloskey, 1985

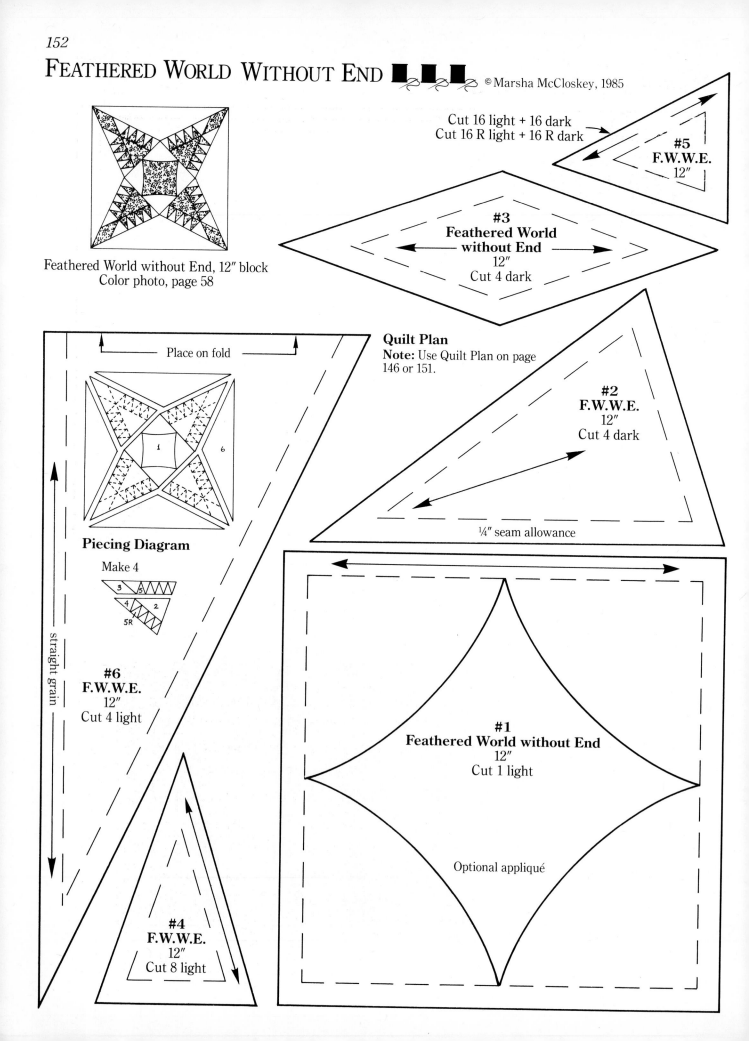

Feathered World without End, 12″ block
Color photo, page 58

Cut 16 light + 16 dark
Cut 16 R light + 16 R dark

#5
F.W.W.E.
12″

#3
Feathered World
without End
12″
Cut 4 dark

Quilt Plan
Note: Use Quilt Plan on page 146 or 151.

#2
F.W.W.E.
12″
Cut 4 dark

¼″ seam allowance

Place on fold

Piecing Diagram

Make 4

3 5
4   2
5R

straight grain

#6
F.W.W.E.
12″
Cut 4 light

#1
Feathered World without End
12″
Cut 1 light

Optional appliqué

#4
F.W.W.E.
12″
Cut 8 light

FOUR-PATCH DIAMOND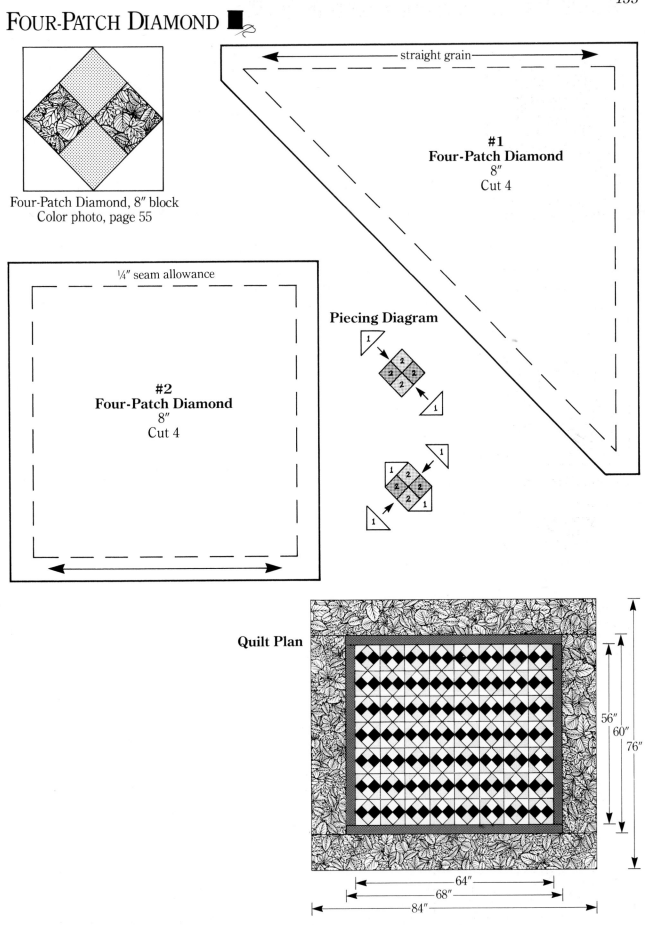

Four-Patch Diamond, 8″ block
Color photo, page 55

¼″ seam allowance

#2
Four-Patch Diamond
8″
Cut 4

straight grain

#1
Four-Patch Diamond
8″
Cut 4

Piecing Diagram

Quilt Plan

56″
60″
76″

64″
68″
84″

HANDS ALL AROUND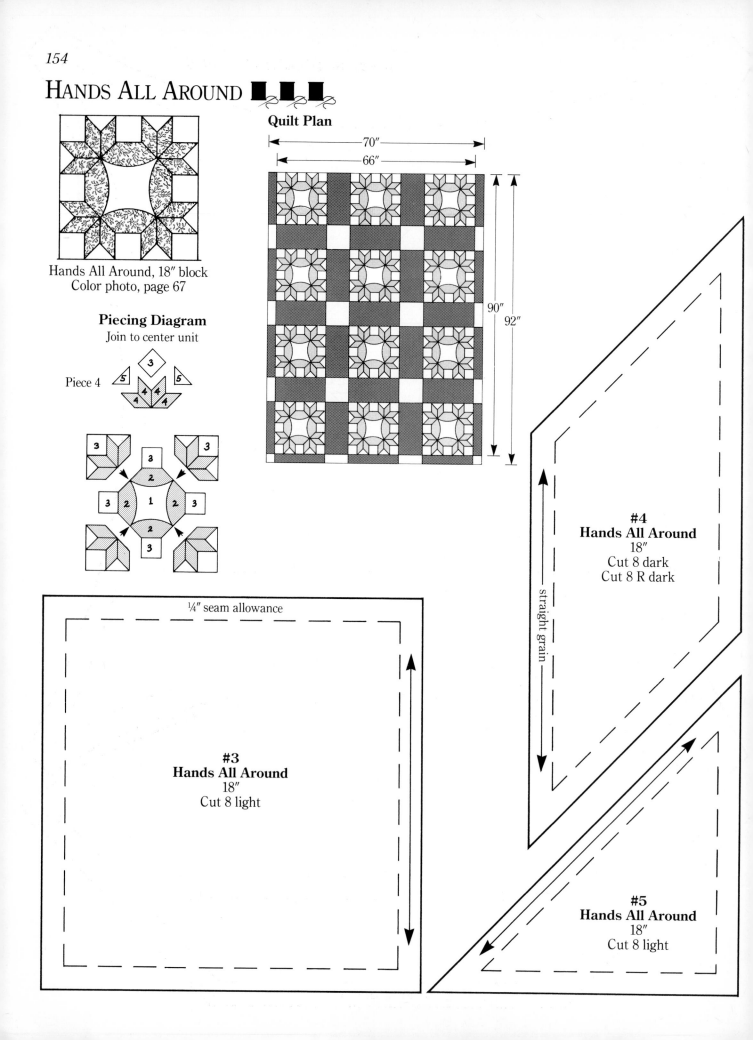

Hands All Around, 18″ block
Color photo, page 67

Quilt Plan

70″

66″

90″

92″

Piecing Diagram

Join to center unit

Piece 4

¼″ seam allowance

#3
Hands All Around
18″
Cut 8 light

#4
Hands All Around
18″
Cut 8 dark
Cut 8 R dark

straight grain

#5
Hands All Around
18″
Cut 8 light

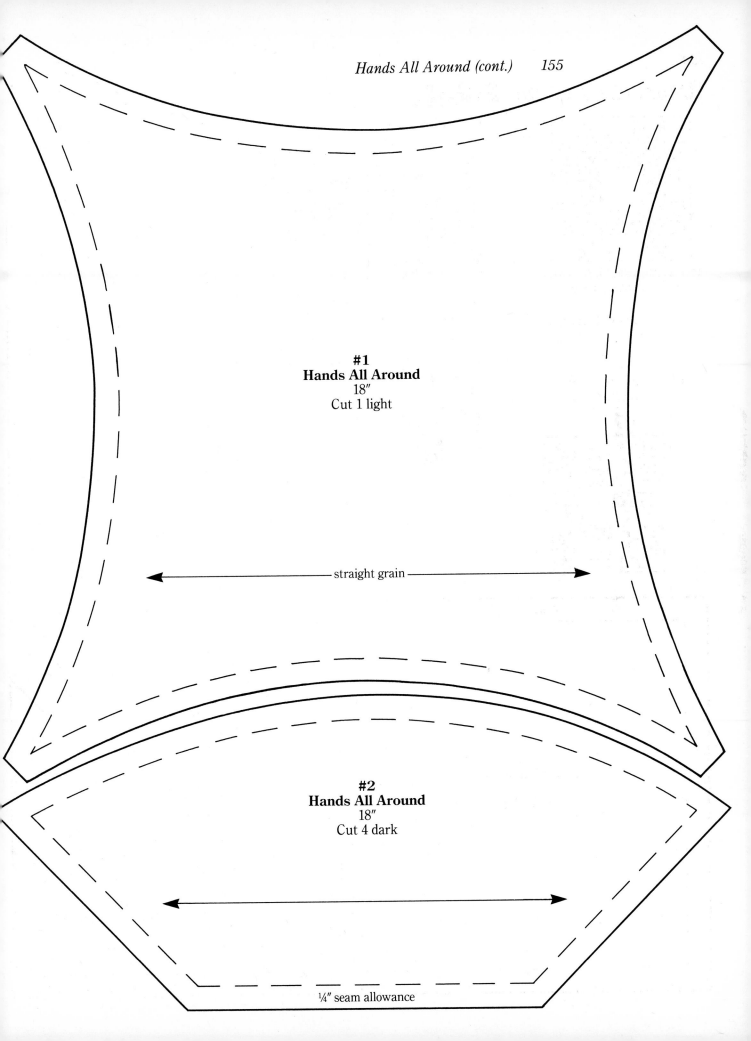

#1
Hands All Around
18″
Cut 1 light

← straight grain →

#2
Hands All Around
18″
Cut 4 dark

¼″ seam allowance

HONEYMOON COTTAGE

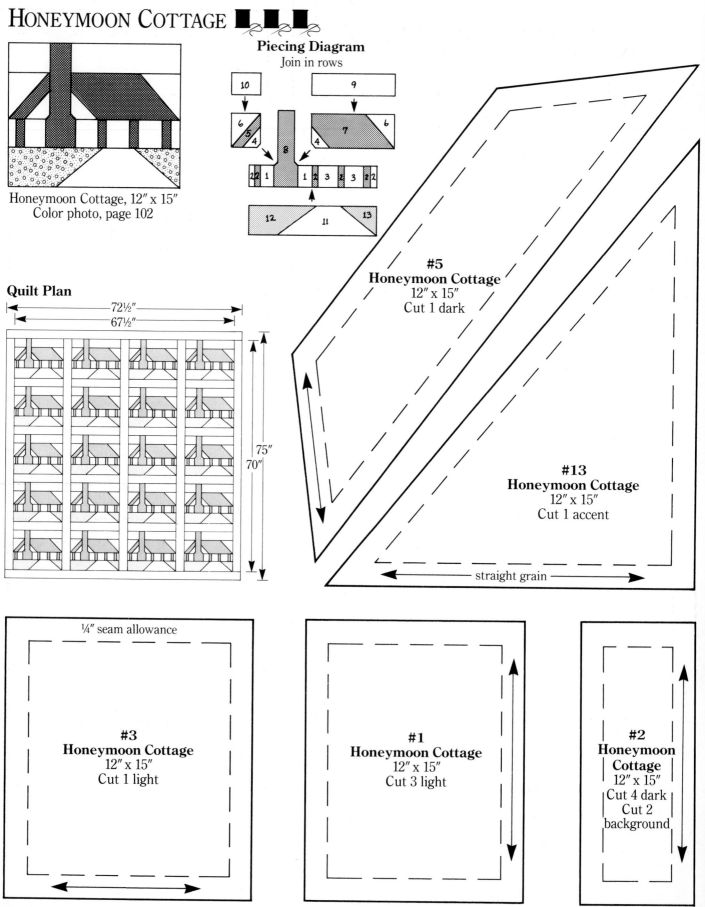

Honeymoon Cottage, 12″ x 15″
Color photo, page 102

Piecing Diagram
Join in rows

Quilt Plan

72½″
67½″

75″
70″

#5
Honeymoon Cottage
12″ x 15″
Cut 1 dark

#13
Honeymoon Cottage
12″ x 15″
Cut 1 accent

straight grain

¼″ seam allowance

#3
Honeymoon Cottage
12″ x 15″
Cut 1 light

#1
Honeymoon Cottage
12″ x 15″
Cut 3 light

#2
Honeymoon Cottage
12″ x 15″
Cut 4 dark
Cut 2 background

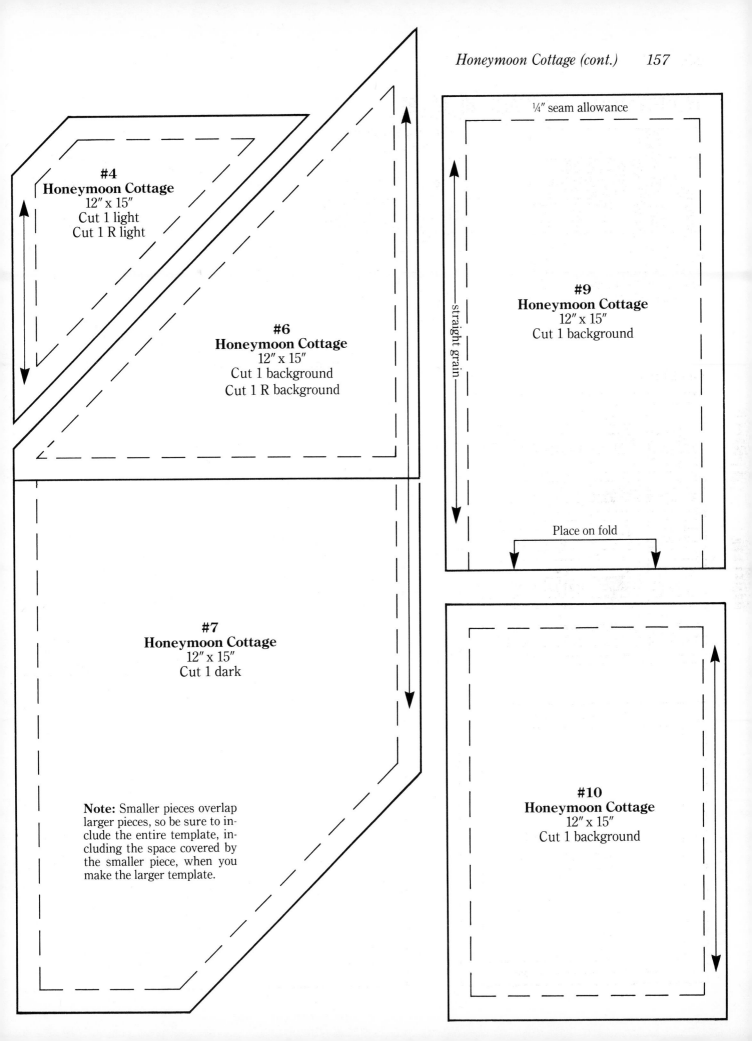

#4
Honeymoon Cottage
12″ x 15″
Cut 1 light
Cut 1 R light

#6
Honeymoon Cottage
12″ x 15″
Cut 1 background
Cut 1 R background

¼″ seam allowance

straight grain

#9
Honeymoon Cottage
12″ x 15″
Cut 1 background

Place on fold

#7
Honeymoon Cottage
12″ x 15″
Cut 1 dark

Note: Smaller pieces overlap larger pieces, so be sure to include the entire template, including the space covered by the smaller piece, when you make the larger template.

#10
Honeymoon Cottage
12″ x 15″
Cut 1 background

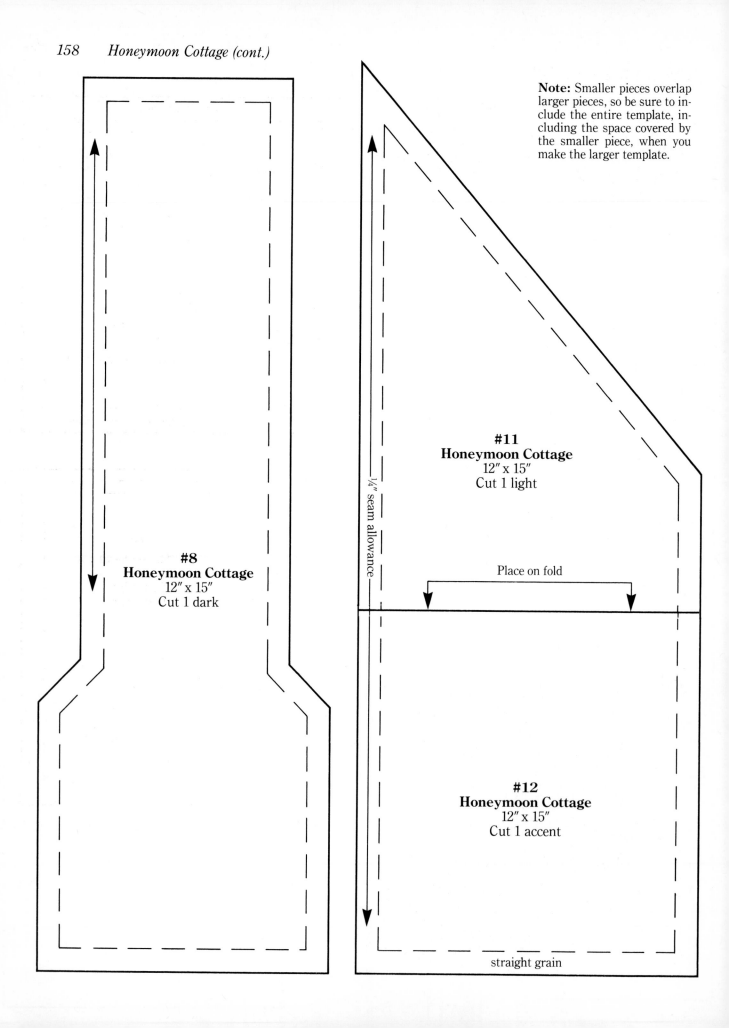

#8
Honeymoon Cottage
12″ x 15″
Cut 1 dark

Note: Smaller pieces overlap larger pieces, so be sure to include the entire template, including the space covered by the smaller piece, when you make the larger template.

#11
Honeymoon Cottage
12″ x 15″
Cut 1 light

¼″ seam allowance

Place on fold

#12
Honeymoon Cottage
12″ x 15″
Cut 1 accent

straight grain

MAPLE LEAF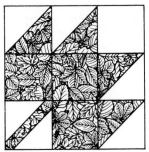

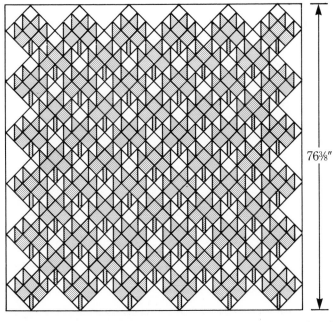

Maple Leaf, 9″ block
Color photo, page 105

For #3 stem, cut 1¼″ x 5″ bias strip (fold and baste to ½″) and position for appliqué on Template #1. Complete appliqué before piecing block.

Piecing Diagram
Join in rows

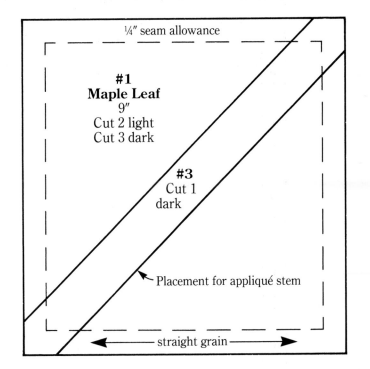

¼″ seam allowance

#1
Maple Leaf
9″
Cut 2 light
Cut 3 dark

#3
Cut 1 dark

← Placement for appliqué stem

←— straight grain —→

#2
Maple Leaf
9″
Cut 4 light
Cut 4 dark

Quilt Plan

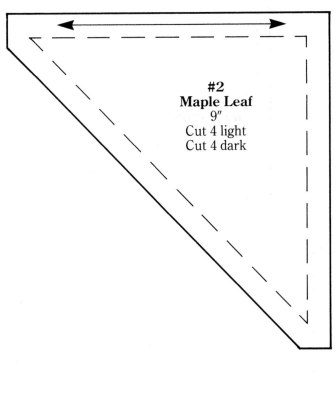

76⅜″

ROLLING STAR ■ ■ ■

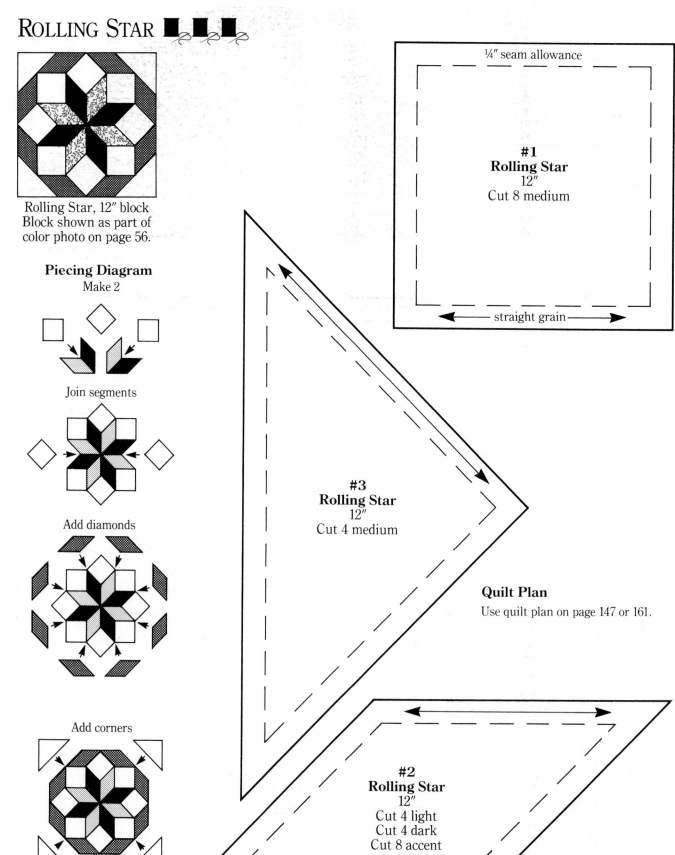

Rolling Star, 12″ block
Block shown as part of
color photo on page 56.

Piecing Diagram
Make 2

Join segments

Add diamonds

Add corners

¼″ seam allowance

**#1
Rolling Star**
12″
Cut 8 medium

straight grain

**#3
Rolling Star**
12″
Cut 4 medium

Quilt Plan

Use quilt plan on page 147 or 161.

**#2
Rolling Star**
12″
Cut 4 light
Cut 4 dark
Cut 8 accent

SISTER'S CHOICE

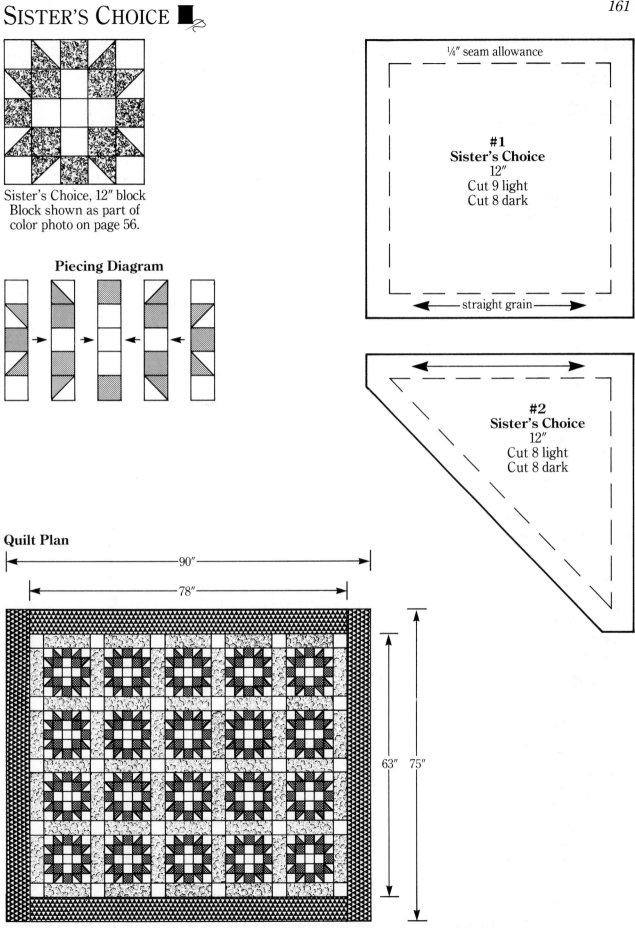

Sister's Choice, 12″ block
Block shown as part of
color photo on page 56.

Piecing Diagram

#1
Sister's Choice
12″
Cut 9 light
Cut 8 dark

¼″ seam allowance

straight grain

#2
Sister's Choice
12″
Cut 8 light
Cut 8 dark

Quilt Plan

90″

78″

63″   75″

STAR AND CRESCENT ■■■

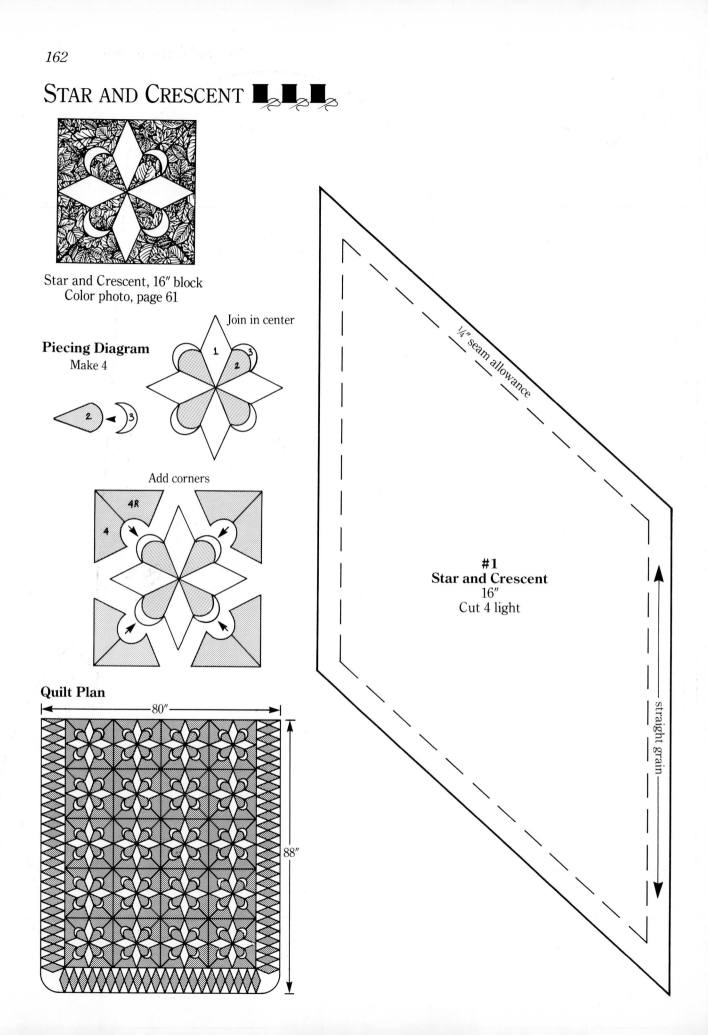

Star and Crescent, 16″ block
Color photo, page 61

Piecing Diagram
Make 4

Join in center

Add corners

Quilt Plan

80″

88″

#1
Star and Crescent
16″
Cut 4 light

¼″ seam allowance

straight grain

P

#2
Star and Crescent
16″
Cut 4 dark

straight grain

#4
Star and Crescent
16″
Cut 4 dark
Cut 4 R dark

¼″ seam allowance

#3
Star and Crescent
16″
Cut 4 light

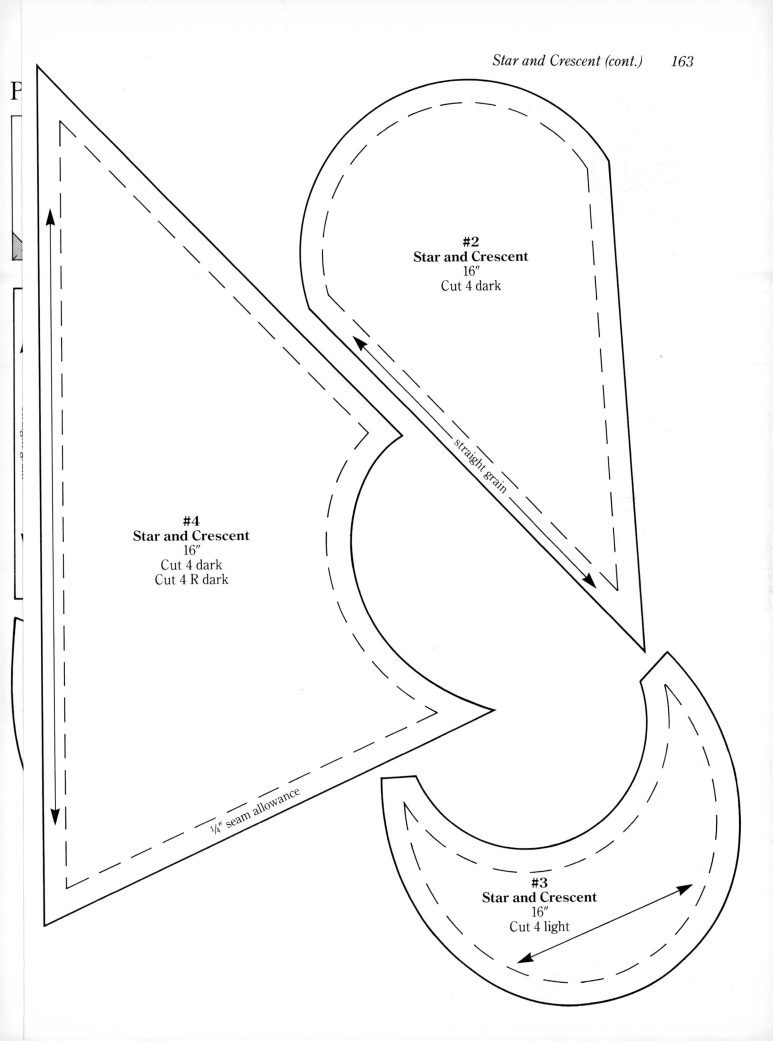

PRESIDENT'S WREATH

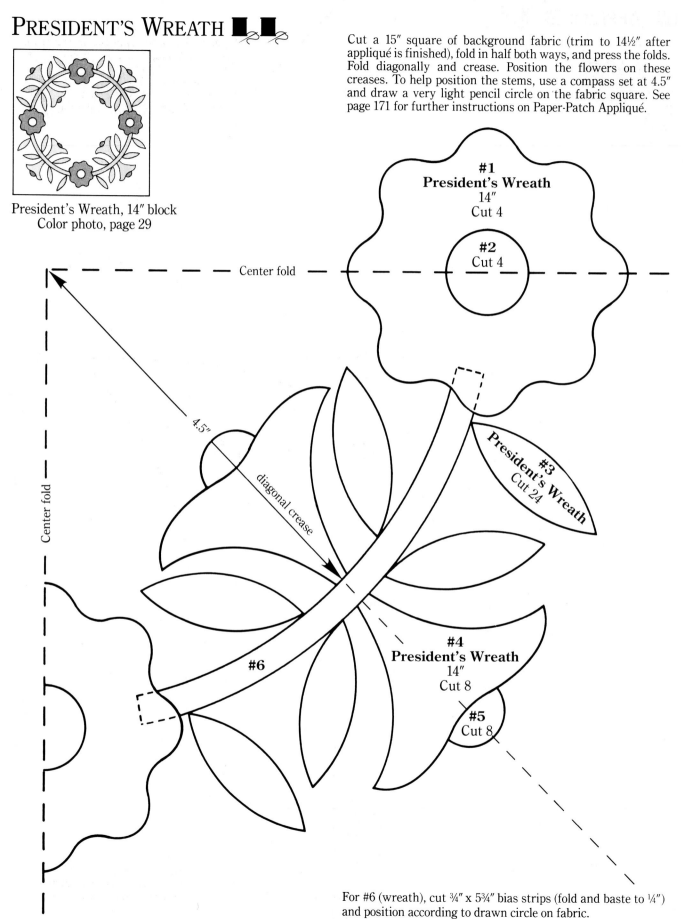

President's Wreath, 14″ block
Color photo, page 29

Cut a 15″ square of background fabric (trim to 14½″ after appliqué is finished), fold in half both ways, and press the folds. Fold diagonally and crease. Position the flowers on these creases. To help position the stems, use a compass set at 4.5″ and draw a very light pencil circle on the fabric square. See page 171 for further instructions on Paper-Patch Appliqué.

#1
President's Wreath
14″
Cut 4

#2
Cut 4

Center fold

4.5″

Center fold

diagonal crease

#3
President's Wreath
Cut 24

#6

#4
President's Wreath
14″
Cut 8

#5
Cut 8

For #6 (wreath), cut ¾″ x 5¾″ bias strips (fold and baste to ¼″) and position according to drawn circle on fabric.

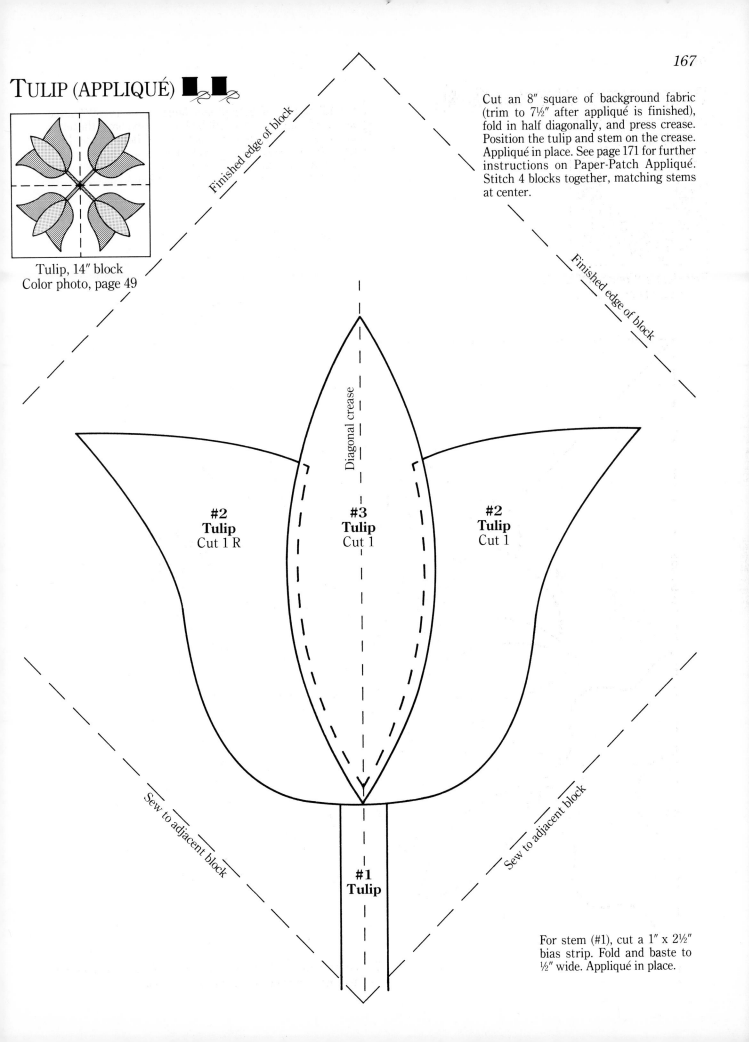

TULIP (APPLIQUÉ)

Tulip, 14″ block
Color photo, page 49

167

Cut an 8″ square of background fabric (trim to 7½″ after appliqué is finished), fold in half diagonally, and press crease. Position the tulip and stem on the crease. Appliqué in place. See page 171 for further instructions on Paper-Patch Appliqué. Stitch 4 blocks together, matching stems at center.

Finished edge of block

Finished edge of block

Diagonal crease

#2
Tulip
Cut 1 R

#3
Tulip
Cut 1

#2
Tulip
Cut 1

Sew to adjacent block

Sew to adjacent block

#1
Tulip

For stem (#1), cut a 1″ x 2½″ bias strip. Fold and baste to ½″ wide. Appliqué in place.

BASIC TECHNIQUES

TOOLS AND SUPPLIES

Drawing Supplies: Graph paper in a ⅛″ grid and colored pencils for drawing quilt plans and sketching design ideas.

Rulers: I use two rulers; both are clear plastic with a red grid of ⅛″ squares. A short ruler is for drawing quilt designs on graph paper; a longer one, 2″ wide and 18″ long, is for drafting designs full size, making templates, measuring borders, and marking quilting lines. If your local quilt shop doesn't carry them, try a stationery store or any place that carries drafting or art supplies. Another useful tool is a 12″ plastic 45°/90° right angle.

Scissors: You will need scissors for paper, a good sharp pair for cutting fabric only, and possibly a little pair for snipping threads. If your fabric scissors are dull, have them sharpened. If they are close to "dead," invest in a new pair. It's worth it.

Template Material: To make templates, you will need graph paper or tracing paper, lightweight posterboard (manila file folders are good) or plastic, and a glue stick.

Markers: Most marking on fabric can be done with a regular #2 lead pencil and a white dressmaker's pencil. Keep them sharp. There is a blue felt-tip marking pen available that is water erasable; it works especially well for marking quilting designs. (When you no longer need the lines for guides, spray them with cool water and the blue marks will disappear.) Ask the salespeople at a local fabric or quilt shop about the different kinds of marking pens available.

Sewing Machine: It needn't be fancy. All you need is an evenly locking straight stitch. Whatever kind of sewing machine you have, get to know it and how it runs. If it needs servicing, have it done, or get out the manual and do it yourself. Replace the old needle with a new one. Often, if your machine

has a zigzag stitch, it will have a throat plate with an oblong hole for the needle to pass through. You might want to replace this plate with one that has a little round hole for straight stitching. This will help eliminate problems you might have with the edges of fabrics being fed into the hole by the action of the feed dog.

Needles: A supply of new sewing machine needles for light- to medium-weight cottons is necessary. A dull or burred needle can snag your fabric or cause uneven stitches. You'll also need an assortment of Sharps for handwork, and quilting needles (Betweens #8, #9, or #10) if you plan to hand quilt.

Pins: Multicolored glass or plastic-headed pins are generally longer, stronger, and easier to see and hold than regular dressmaker's pins.

Iron and Ironing Board: An iron with a shot of steam is useful.

FABRIC REQUIREMENTS

To get a "ball-park" figure or rough estimate of the fabric needed for a quilt, first figure the yardage for the quilt backing. For example, a finished quilt 80″ x 104″ would require six yards of fabric for the backing: two 3-yard lengths (108″) of 45″-wide fabric, seamed down the middle to get the 80″ width. Then, multiply the amount of fabric needed for the backing (six yards in this case) by 1.5.

$$6 \text{ yards} \times 1.5 = 9 \text{ yards}$$

Nine yards is a conservative rough estimate of fabric needed for the quilt top. Use it for reference. The amount of fabric you actually need will probably be a bit more. Figure the yardage as outlined below, then look at the total. Is it close to your rough estimate? If your calculations total 3½ yards (nowhere near nine yards), you'll know there is something wrong. Likewise, a

40-yard total is unreasonable. Ten yards or 11½ yards, however, is in the ball park.

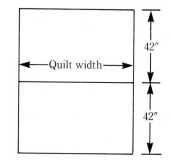

Seam fabric together for quilt backing

To figure specific yardage requirements, you will need a quilt plan. This is generally a scale drawing on graph paper that shows unit block design and size, type of set and number of set pieces, and indicates border treatment and dimensions. Sample quilt plans are given with each block pattern.

Base yardage requirements on a good quilt plan and follow these steps.

1. Identify and make templates for all the shapes in the quilt design, i.e., pieces in the patterned blocks and the set pieces (lattices or alternate blocks). You don't have to make templates for larger border pieces; knowing their dimensions is enough.

   Each template is identified by the block name and size. All templates for the blocks are labeled with the template number, block name, and the number of pieces to be cut for one block, except where noted.

2. For each template, write the number of pieces to be cut from each fabric in your design. Cutting directions will sometimes specify that a template be reversed, so that a "mirror image" is cut. Cut the first piece with the template face up, then flip it over face down to cut the reversed piece.

3. Armed with shapes, sizes, and numbers, proceed to figure out how

many of each template will fit on the usable width of the fabric. With fabric that is 45″ on the bolt, you will generally have a usable width of only 42″. Selvages should be cut off, and you must allow for some shrinkage. For example, twelve 8½″ squares are needed as set pieces in the quilt plan. Dividing 42″ by 8.5″, you find that four complete squares can be cut from the width of the fabric. Each set of four squares requires 8.5″ of the fabric length. To cut twelve squares, multiply 3 x 8.5″ and you find that you need 25.5″ of the fabric length. This is nearly ¾ yard (27″), but buying only ¾ yard would be cutting it close. I would go on to the next highest eighth of a yard and buy ⅞ yard. It is a good idea to buy at least four extra inches of a fabric to allow for shrinkage, straightening, and cutting mistakes.

Complete this process for each shape and fabric in the quilt plan. Total the amounts and compare with your ball-park figure. If it seems reasonable, you are ready to buy fabric.

CUTTING

Trim the selvage from the fabric before you begin cutting. When one fabric is to be used both for borders and in the unit block designs, cut the borders first and the smaller pieces from what is left over.

At the ironing board, press and fold the fabric so that one, two, or four layers can be cut at one time (except for linear prints, such as stripes and checks, that should be cut one at a time). Fold the fabric so that each piece will be cut on the straight grain.

Position stiffened templates on the fabric so the arrows match the straight grain of the fabric. With a sharp pencil (white for dark fabrics, lead for light ones), trace around the template on the fabric. This is the cutting line. Cut just inside this line to most accurately duplicate the template.

In machine piecing, there are no drawn lines to guide your sewing. The seam line is ¼″ from the cut edge of the fabric, so this outside edge must be precisely cut to ensure accurate sewing.

MACHINE PIECING

For machine piecing, use white or neutral thread as light in color as the lightest fabric in the project. Use a dark neutral thread for piecing dark solids. It is easier to work with 100% cotton thread on some machines. Check your needle. If it is dull, burred, or bent, replace it with a new one.

Sew exact ¼″ seams. To determine the ¼″ seam allowance on your machine, place a template under the presser foot and gently lower the needle onto the seam line. The distance from the needle to the edge of the template is ¼″. Lay a piece of masking tape at the edge of the template to act as the ¼″ mark; use the edge as a guide. Stitch length should be set at 10–12 stitches per inch. For most of the sewing in this book, sew from cut edge to cut edge (exceptions will be noted). Backtack, if you wish, although it is really unnecessary as each seam will be crossed and held by another.

Use chain piecing whenever possible to save time and thread. To chain piece, sew one seam, but do not lift the presser foot. Do not take the piece out of the sewing machine and do not cut the thread. Instead, set up the next piece to be sewn and continue stitching. There will be a little twist of thread between the two pieces. Sew all the seams you can at one time in this way, then remove the "chain." Clip the threads.

Press the seam allowances to one side, toward the darker fabric when possible. Avoid too much ironing as you sew because it tends to stretch biases and distort fabric shapes.

To piece a block, sew the smallest pieces together first to form units. Join smaller units to form larger ones until the block is complete.

Short seams need not be pinned unless matching is involved, or the

seam is longer than 4″. Keep pins away from the seam line. Sewing over pins tends to burr the needle and makes it hard to be accurate in tight places.

Here are six matching techniques that can be helpful in many different piecing situations.

1. **Opposing Seams:** When stitching one seamed unit to another, press seam allowances on the seams that need to match in opposite directions. The two "opposing" seams will hold each other in place and evenly distribute the bulk. Plan pressing to take advantage of opposing seams.

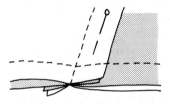

2. **Positioning Pin:** A pin, carefully pushed straight through two points that need to match and pulled tight, will establish the proper point of matching. Pin the seam normally and remove the positioning pin before stitching.

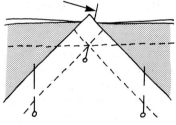

Positioning pin

3. **The X:** When triangles are pieced, stitches will form an X at the next seam line. Stitch through the center of the X to make sure the points on the sewn triangles will not be chopped off.

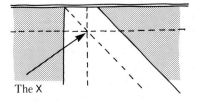

The X

4. **Easing:** When two pieces to be sewn together are slightly different lengths, pin the points of matching and stitch with the shorter piece on top. The feed dog will ease the fullness of the bottom piece.

5. **Set-in seams:** Set-in seams are used where three seams come together at an angle.

   a. Sew a diamond to a triangle or square. With triangle or square on top, begin to sew at the ¼" seam line. Backtack by sewing two stitches forward and two stitches back, taking care not to stitch into the seam allowance. (Backtacking is necessary here to hold the stitches, as they will not be crossed and held by another line of stitching.) Sew the remainder of the seam, ending at the cut edge of the fabric. (No backtacking is necessary here, as this seam will be crossed and held by another.)

   b. Sew the second diamond to the same triangle or square. With the triangle or square on top, sew from the outside edge of the fabric, ending with a backtack at the ¼" seam line.

   c. Folding the triangle or square out of the way, match the points of the diamonds to position them

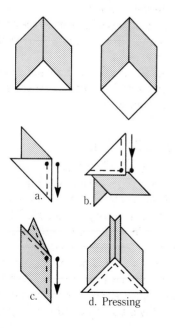

a.
b.
c.
d. Pressing

for the third seam. Stitch the diamonds together, beginning with a backtack at the inner ¼" seam line and ending at the raw edge of the fabric.

   d. With an iron, lightly press the center seam open. Press the other two seams toward the diamonds. (Sometimes, especially when working with fabric that has a low thread count, it is better to finger press while piecing to avoid stretching bias edges. Use the iron only to press the finished block.)

6. **Curved Seams:**

   a. Find the center of each piece by folding it in half and making a crease.

   b. Match the centers of the pieces and pin.

   c. Utilizing points trimmed for easy matching, pin the two ends.

   d. With the convex curved piece underneath and the concave piece on top, carefully stitch the ¼" seam, matching the fabric edges along the curve as you go.

   e. After sewing the seams, press them away from the center.

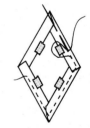

a.
b.
c.
d.

7. **Making Eight Points Come Together:** Making eight points come together crisply is important in the Envelope block and many others.

   a. Chain piece light and dark triangles together to form four squares. Press each seam toward the dark.

   b. Make two halves of the pinwheel by sewing two square units together, as shown. Match, using opposing diagonal seams. Press each new seam toward the dark.

   c. Sew the center seam. Match, using positioning pin and opposing seams. Stitch exactly through the **X**.

ENGLISH PAPER-PIECING METHOD

1. Pin the center of a paper template to wrong side of fabric. Fold fabric edge over template and secure with tape.

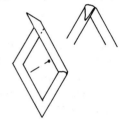

2. Baste all around the patch through the fabric and paper; then, carefully remove the masking tape.

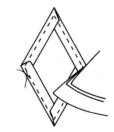

3. Press the fabric folds—this makes sewing the patches much easier.

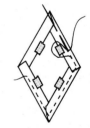

4. Join individual patches together with tiny overcasting stitches.

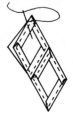

5. Join the patches into rows with overcasting stitches.

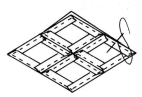

PAPER-PATCH APPLIQUÉ

In paper-patch appliqué, a stiff paper forms a base around which the fabric is shaped.

1. Trace each appliqué shape on stiff paper. (The subscription cards that come in magazines are the perfect weight. At last there is a use for those cards!)
2. Cut out a paper template for each shape in the appliqué design. Do not add seam allowances.
3. Pin each template to the wrong side of your appliqué fabric.

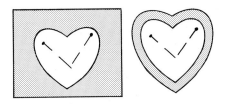

4. Cut out the fabric in the template shape, adding ¼″ seam allowance.
5. With your fingers, fold the seam allowance over the edge of the paper and baste it to the paper.
   a. Start with deep cleavages and inside curves. Clip these areas close to the paper to allow the fabric to stretch over the template.
   b. On outside curves, take small running stitches in the fabric only. This will allow you to ease the fullness over the template.

c. Use running stitches to baste a circle.

d. Points require some encouragement to lie flat and come to a sharp point. First, fold the tip over the paper; then, hold it in place while you fold the right side across the tip. Use a small, sharp scissors to cut away the extra fabric. Next, fold the left seam across the right one and trim it. Take two tiny basting stitches through the folds, including the paper, to hold everything in place.

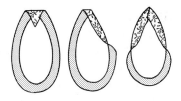

6. When all seam allowances have been basted onto the templates, press them with an iron.
7. Machine baste the shapes in position on the quilt block.
8. Use a blind stitch to appliqué the pieces to the quilt block (see following section). Complete the appliqué; then remove the basting stitches.
9. Working from the back of the quilt block, carefully snip the background fabric behind each shape and remove the paper. Some quiltmakers prefer to remove the paper from the front of the work before the appliqué stitching is completed. Leave a small (about 1½″), straight section unstitched. Remove the basting threads. Pull the paper out through the opening and complete the stitching.

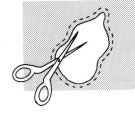

BLIND STITCH

1. Use a single thread, about 20″ long, that is the same color as the shape you are sewing. For example, use green thread for a green leaf.
2. Thread the needle and tie a knot.
3. Hold the needle in your right hand and hold the quilt block in your left hand. (Reverse this if you are left-handed.)
4. Bring the needle around to the back (wrong side) of the block.
5. Insert the needle through the background fabric and through the very edge of the appliqué fabric. (Your needle will nick the edge of the paper template as it goes through the fabric; that is fine.) Pull the thread all the way through.
6. Insert the needle through the background fabric only, just behind the previous stitch.

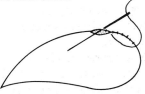

7. Tilt the needle and come up about ⅛″ from previous stitch through both layers. It is usually easier for right-handed people to work counterclockwise and for left-handed people to work clockwise.
8. Continue sewing around the edges, making your stitches as invisible as possible.
9. At the end of your thread, take a few tiny backstitches on the back of your work.

SETTING THE QUILT TOGETHER

When all of the blocks are pieced, you are ready to "set" the quilt top together, following a quilt plan. First, stitch blocks, or blocks and lattices, together into rows, using ¼″ seams. Then, stitch rows of blocks, or rows of blocks and lattice strips, together. Setting sequences are shown in diagrams.

When the center portion is pieced

together, borders may then be added to the quilt.

Assembly sequence with lattices

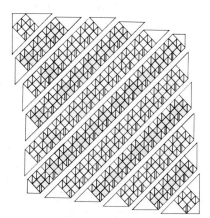

Assembly sequence of diagonally set quilt

MITERING CORNERS

1. Determine the finished outside dimensions of your quilt. Cut the borders this length, plus ½″ for seam allowances. When using a striped fabric for the borders, make sure the design on all four borders is cut the same way. Multiple borders should be sewn together and the resulting "striped" units treated as a single border for mitering.

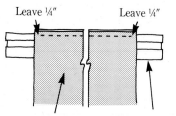

Center (wrong side)   Border unit made of 3 fabric strips (right side)

2. To attach the border to the pieced section of the quilt, center each border on a side so the ends extend equally on either side of the center section. Using a ¼″ seam allowance, sew the border to the center, leaving ¼″ unsewn at the beginning and end of the stitching line. Press the seam allowances toward the border.

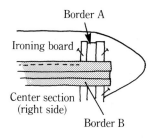

Border A
Ironing board
Center section (right side)
Border B

3. Arrange the first corner to be mitered on the ironing board, as illustrated. Press the corner flat and straight. To prevent it from slipping, pin the quilt to the ironing board. Following the illustration, turn Border B right side up, folding the corner to be mitered under at a 45° angle. Match the raw edges underneath with those of Border A. Fuss with it until it looks good. The stripes and border designs should meet. Check the squareness of the corner with a right angle. Press the fold, which will be the sewing line. Pin the borders together to prevent shifting and unpin the piece from the board. Turn wrong side out and pin along the fold line, readjusting if necessary to match the designs.

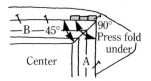

4. Machine baste from the inside to the outside corner on the fold line, leaving ¼″ at the beginning unsewn. Check for accuracy. If it is right, sew again with a regular stitch. Backtack at the beginning and end of the stitching line. (After you have mitered several times, the basting step ceases to be necessary.)

Trim the excess fabric ¼″ along the mitered seam. Press this seam open. Press the other seams to the outside.

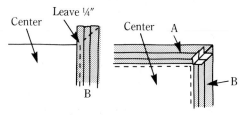

PREPARING TO QUILT

Marking

In most cases, the quilt top must be marked with lines to guide stitching before you quilt. Where you place the quilting lines will depend on the patchwork design, the type of batting used, and how much quilting you want to do.

Try to avoid quilting too close to the seam lines, where the bulk of seam allowances might slow you down or make the stitches uneven. Keep in mind that the purpose of quilting, besides its aesthetic value, is to securely hold the three layers together. Don't leave large areas unquilted.

Thoroughly press the quilt top and mark it before you assemble it with the batting and backing. You will need marking pencils, a long ruler or yardstick, stencils or templates for quilting motifs, and a smooth, clean, hard surface on which to work. Use a sharp marking pencil and lightly mark the quilting lines on the fabric. No matter what kind of marking tool you use, light lines will be easier to remove than heavy ones.

Backing

A single length of 45″-wide fabric often can be used for backing small quilts. To be safe, plan on a usable width of only 42″ after shrinkage and cutting off selvages. For larger quilts, you will need to sew two lengths of fabric together to have a backing large enough.

Cut the backing an inch larger than the quilt top all the way around.

Press thoroughly with seams open. Lay the backing face down on a large, clean, flat surface. With masking tape, tape the backing down (without stretching) to keep it smooth and flat while you are working with the other layers.

Batting

Batting is the filler in a quilt or comforter. Thick batting is used in comforters that are tied. If you plan to quilt, use thin batting and quilt by hand.

Thin batting comes in 100% polyester, 100% cotton, and a cotton-polyester (80%–20%) combination. All-cotton batting requires close quilting to prevent shifting and separating in the wash. Most old quilts have cotton batting and are rather flat. Cotton is a good natural fiber that lasts well and is compatible with cotton and cotton-blend fabrics. Less quilting is required on 100% polyester batting. If polyester batting is glazed or bonded, it is easy to work with, won't pull apart, and has more loft than cotton.

Assembling the Layers

Center the freshly ironed and marked quilt top on top of the batting, face up. Starting in the middle, pin baste the three layers together while gently smoothing out fullness to the sides and corners. Take care not to distort the straight lines of the quilt design and the borders.

After pinning, baste the layers together with needle and light-colored thread. Start in the middle and make a line of large stitches to each corner to

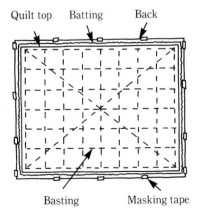

Quilt top   Batting   Back

Basting   Masking tape

form a large X. Continue basting in a grid of parallel lines 6″–8″ apart. Finish with a row of basting around the outside edges. Quilts to be quilted with a hoop or on your lap will be handled more than those quilted on a frame; therefore, quilts in a hoop will require more basting.

After basting, remove the pins. Now you are ready to quilt.

HAND QUILTING

To quilt by hand, you will need quilting thread, quilting needles, small scissors, a thimble, and perhaps a balloon or large rubber band to help grasp the needle if it gets stuck. Quilt on a frame, a large hoop, or just on your lap or a table. Use a single strand of quilting thread no longer than 18″. Make a small single knot in the end of the thread. The quilting stitch is a small running stitch that goes through all three layers of the quilt. Take two, three, or even four stitches at a time if you can keep them even. When crossing seams, you might find it necessary to "hunt and peck" one stitch at a time.

To begin, insert the needle in the top layer about ¾″ from the point you want to start stitching. Pull the needle out at the starting point and gently tug at the knot until it pops through the fabric and is buried in the batting. Make a backstitch and begin quilting. Stitches should be tiny (8–10 per inch is good), even, and straight. At first, concentrate on even and straight; tiny will come with practice.

When you come almost to the end of the thread, make a single knot fairly close to the fabric. Take a backstitch to bury the knot in the batting. Run the thread off through the batting and out the quilt top. Snip it off. The first and last stitches look different from the running stitches between. To make them less noticeable, start and stop

Hand quilting stitch

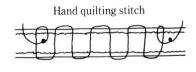

where quilting lines cross each other or at seam joints.

BINDING THE EDGES

After quilting, trim excess batting and backing even with the edge of the quilt top. A rotary cutter and long ruler will ensure accurate straight edges. If basting from hand quilting is no longer in place, baste all three layers together.

1. Cut 2¼″ wide bias strips for binding. Seam ends together to make a long continuous strip. Press in half, wrong sides together, to make a "double" binding.

2. Using a ¼″ seam allowance, sew the binding strips to the front of the quilt, sewing through all layers. Be careful not to stretch the bias or the quilt edge as you sew. Stitch until you reach the seam-line point at the corner. Backstitch; cut threads.

3. Turn quilt to prepare for sewing along the next edge. Fold binding away from the quilt, as shown; then, fold again to place binding along edge of quilt. This fold creates an angled pleat at the corner.

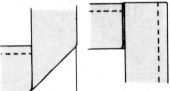

4. Stitch from the fold of the binding to the seam line of the adjacent edge. Backstitch; cut threads. Fold binding as in step 2 and continue around edge.

5. Join the beginning and ending of the binding strip, or plan to hand sew one end to overlap the other.

6. Turn binding to the back side and blindstitch in place. At each corner, fold binding in the sequence shown to form a miter on the back of quilt.

Fold second

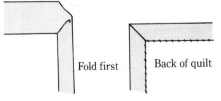

Fold first   Back of quilt

NOTES

1. White, *Quilts and Counterpanes in the Newark Museum,* p. 3.
2. Binney, *Homage to Amanda,* p. 48.
3. Colby, *Patchwork,* p. 28.
4. Ibid., p. 30.
5. Ibid., pp. 23–24.
6. Carlisle, *Quilts at Shelburne Museum,* p. 48.
7. Dunton, *Old Quilts,* p. 43.
8. McKim, *101 Patchwork Patterns,* p. 72.
9. Roan and Gehret, *Just a Quilt,* p. 9.
10. Brackman, *An Encyclopedia of Quilt Patterns,* p. 14.
11. Rae, *The Quilts of the British Isles,* p. 26.
12. Colby, *Patchwork,* p. 58.
13. Roan and Gehret, *Just a Quilt,* p. 26.
14. Ibid., p. 36.
15. Fagan Affleck, *Just New from the Mills,* p. 89.
16. Colby, *Patchwork,* p. 30.
17. McKim, *101 Patchwork Patterns,* p. 5.
18. Bullard and Shelly, *Chintz Quilts,* p. 20.
19. Nicoll, *Quilted for Friends,* p. 5.
20. Carlisle, *Quilts at Shelburne Museum,* p. 87.
21. Dunton, *Old Quilts,* pp. 17–18.
22. Nicoll, *Quilted for Friends,* p. 34.
23. Taylor, *The Story of Kennett,* p. 52.
24. Finley, *Old Patchwork Quilts and the Women Who Made Them,* p. 192.
25. Mainardi, *Quilts: The Great American Art,* pp. 3, 9.
26. Finley, *Old Patchwork Quilts,* p. 39.
27. Ibid., pp. 31–38.
28. Colby, *Patchwork Quilts,* p. 66.
29. Finley, *Old Patchwork Quilts,* p. 148.
30. Brackman, "Leaves and Foliage," *Quilter's Newsletter Magazine,* October 1989, p. 36.
31. Bonfield, *The Production of Cloth, Clothing and Quilts,* p. 78.
32. Fagan Affleck, *Just New from the Mills,* p. 55.
33. Peto, *Historic Quilts,* p. 17.
34. Orlofsky, *Quilts in America,* p. 49.
35. McKendry, *Traditional Quilts and Bed Coverings,* p. 103.
36. Holstein, *The Pieced Quilt,* p. 85.
37. Smith, "Quilt Blocks—or—Quilt Patterns," *Uncoverings 1986,* p. 102.
38. Reprints of the original Ladies Art Company watercolors and patterns recently discovered by Harold and Dorothymae Groves are available from Groves Publishing, PO Box 5370, Kansas City, MO 64131.
39. Benberry, "Ladies Art Company, Pioneer in Printed Patterns," *Nimble Needle Treasures,* Spring 1971, p. 4.
40. Benberry, "The Twentieth Century's First Quilt Revival," *Quilter's Newsletter Magazine,* October 1979, p. 10.
41. Woodard and Greenstein, *Twentieth Century American Quilts,* p. 5. Appointments can be made to view this valuable design resource.
42. Stearns and Foster, *Blue Book of Quilts,* p. 23.
43. Nephew, *My Mother's Quilts,* p. 17.
44. Woodard and Greenstein, *Twentieth Century American Quilts,* p. 8
45. Ibid., p. 35.
46. Benberry, "The Twentieth Century's First Quilt Revival," *Quilter's Newsletter Magazine,* September 1979, p. 29.
47. Benberry, "The Twentieth Century's First Quilt Revival," *Quilter's Newsletter Magazine,* September 1979, pp. 25–26.
48. Woodard and Greenstein, *Twentieth Century American Quilts,* pp. 11–12.
49. Gross, "Cuesta Benberry: Part II—Significant Milestones for Quilters," *Quilters Journal,* no. 24, p. 24.
50. Woodard and Greenstein, *Twentieth Century American Quilts,* pp. 34–35.
51. McKim, *101 Patchwork Patterns,* p. 97.
52. Mainardi, *Quilts: The Great American Art,* p. 6.
53. Finley, *Old Patchwork Quilts,* p. 132.
54. Carroll, *Patchwork and Appliqué,* p. 54.

BIBLIOGRAPHY

Bacon, Lenice Ingram. *American Patchwork Quilts.* New York: William Morrow and Co., Inc., 1973.

Benberry, Cuesta. "Ladies Art Company, Pioneer in Printed Patterns." *Nimble Needle Treasures* (Spring 1971), p. 4.

————. "The Twentieth Century's First Quilt Revival." *Quilter's Newsletter Magazine* (September 1979), p. 29.

————. "The Twentieth Century's First Quilt Revival." *Quilter's Newsletter Magazine* (October 1979), p. 10.

Beyer, Jinny. *Medallion Quilts.* McClean, Va.: E. P. M. Publications, 1982.

Binney, Edwin, and Binney-Winslow, Gail. *Homage to Amanda.* San Francisco: R. K. Press, 1984.

Bonfield, Lynn A. "The Production of Cloth, Clothing, and Quilts in Ninteenth Century New England Homes." *Uncoverings 1981,* p. 78.

Brackman, Barbara. *An Encyclopedia of Pieced Quilt Patterns.* Lawrence, Kans.: Prairie Flower Publishing, 1979.

————. "Leaves and Foliage." *Quilter's Newsletter Magazine* (October 1989), pp. 36–37.

Bullard, Lacy Fulmar, and Schiell, Betty Jo. *Chintz Quilts: Unfading Glory.* Tallahassee, Fla.: Serendipity Publishers, 1983.

Carlisle, Lilian Baker. *Pieced Work and Appliqué Quilts at Shelburne Museum.* Shelburne, Va.: The Shelburne Museum, Inc., 1957.

Carroll, Amy, ed. *Patchwork and Appliqué.* London: Dorling Kindersley, Ltd., 1981.

Colby, Averil. *Patchwork.* London: Batsford, Ltd., 1958.

————. *Patchwork Quilts.* London: Batsford, Ltd., 1965.

Dubois, Jean. *Ann Orr Patchwork.* Durango, Colo.: La Plata Press, 1977.

Dunton, William Rush, Jr., M.D. *Old Quilts.* Catonsville, Md.: William Rush Dunton, Jr., M.D., 1946.

Fagan Affleck, Diane L. *Just New from the Mills: Printed Cottons in America.* North Andover, Mass.: Museum of American Textile History, 1987.

Field, June. *Creative Patchwork.* London: Sir Isaac Pitman and Sons, Ltd., 1974.

Finley, Ruth E. *Old Patchwork Quilts and the Women Who Made Them.* Newton Center, Mass.: Charles T. Branford Company, 1929.

Gross, Joyce. "Cuesta Benberry: Part II—Significant Milestones for Quilters." *Quilters Journal,* no. 24 (1984), p. 24.

Groves, Harold and Dorothymae. *Ladies Art Company, Sets 1-63.* Kansas City, Mo.: Groves Publishing, 1988.

————. *The Kansas City Star Classic Quilt Patterns, Volumes 1-10.* Kansas City, Mo.: Groves Publishing, 1988.

Hagerman, Betty J. *A Meeting of the Sunbonnet Children.* Baldwin City, Kans.: Betty J. Hagerman, 1979.

Hall, Carrie A., and Kretsinger, Rose G. *The Romance of the Patchwork Quilt.* New York: Bonanza Books, 1935.

Holstein, Jonathan. *The Pieced Quilt: An American Design Tradition.* Greenwich, Conn.: New York Graphic Society, Ltd., 1973.

Katzenberg, Dena. *Baltimore Album Quilts.* Baltimore, Md.: Baltimore Museum of Art, 1981.

Kile, Michael M., ed. *The Quilt Digest — 1.* San Francisco: Quilt Digest Press, 1983.

————. *The Quilt Digest — 3.* San Francisco: Quilt Digest Press, 1985.

Lazansky, Jennette. *In the Heart of Pennsylvania.* Lewisburg, Pa.: Oral Traditions Project of the Union County Historical Society, 1985.

————. *Pieced by Mother.* Lewisburg, Pa.: Oral Traditions Project of the Union County Historical Society, 1987.

Mainardi, Patricia. *Quilts: The Great American Art.* Pedro, Calif.: Miles & Weir, Ltd., 1978.

Martin, Judy. *Shining Star Quilts.* Denver, Colo.: Leman Publications, 1987.

Martin, Nancy J. *Pieces of the Past.* Bothell, Wash.: That Patchwork Place, Inc., 1986.

McKendry, Ruth. *Traditional Quilts and Bed Coverings.* New York: Van Nostrand Reinhold Co., 1979.

McKim, Ruby. *101 Patchwork Patterns.* New York: Dover Publications, Inc., 1962.

Nelson, Cyril I., and Houck, Carter. *The Quilt Engagement Calendar Treasury.* New York: E. P. Dutton, 1982.

Nephew, Sara. *My Mother's Quilts.* Bothell, Wash.: That Patchwork Place, Inc., 1988.

Nicoll, Jessica F. *Quilted for Friends.* Wintethur, Del.: Wintethur Museum, 1986.

Orlofsky, Patsy and Myron. *Quilts in America.* New York: McGraw Hill Book Co., 1974.

Parry, Linda, ed. *A Practical Guide to Patchwork from the Victoria and Albert Collection.* London: Unwin Hyman, 1987.

Peto, Florence. *Historic Quilts.* New York: The American Historical Company, 1939.

Pettit, Florence H. *America's Printed and Painted Fabrics.* New York: Hastings House, 1970.

Prudence, Penny. *Old Time Quilts.* Seattle: Seattle Post Intelligencer, 1927.

Rae, Janet. *The Quilts of the British Isles.* New York: E. P. Dutton, 1987.

Ramsey, Bets, and Waldvogel, MeriKay. *The Quilts of Tennessee.* Nashville: Rutledge Hill Press, 1986.

Roan, Nancy, and Gehret, Ellen J. *Just a Quilt.* Green Lane, Pa.: Goschenhoppen Historians, Inc., 1984.

Rowley, Nancy J. "Red Cross Quilts for the Great War." *Uncoverings 1982,* pp. 43-50.

Sienkiewicz, Eleanor. *Baltimore Beauties and Beyond.* Lafayette, Calif.: C & T Publishing, 1989.

Smith, Wilene. "Quilt Blocks or Quilt Patterns." *Uncoverings 1986,* p. 102.

The 1957 Mountain Mist Blue Book of Quilts. Cincinnati: Stearns and Foster Company, 1956.

Taylor, Bayard. *The Story of Kennett.* Bayard Taylor, 1894.

Troianello, Ann (Project Chairman). *A Common Thread: Quilts in the Yakima Valley.* Yakima, Wash.: Yakima Valley Museum and Historical Association, 1985.

Walker, Michelle. *Quilting and Patchwork.* London: Dorling Kindersley Ltd., 1983.

Webster, Marie D. *Quilts: Their Story and How to Make Them.* Garden City, N.Y.: Doubleday, 1916.

White, Margaret E. *Quilts and Counterpanes in the Newark Museum.* Newark, N.J.: Newark Museum, 1948.

Woodard, Thomas K., and Greenstein, Blanche. *Twentieth Century American Quilts.* New York: E. P. Dutton, 1988.

INDEX OF PATTERNS

THAT PATCHWORK PLACE PUBLICATIONS

Angelsong by Joan Vibert
Baby Quilts from Grandma by Carolann Palmer
Back to Square One by Nancy J. Martin
A Banner Year by Nancy J. Martin
Basket Garden by Mary Hickey
Christmas Memories—A Folk Art Celebration
     by Nancy J. Martin
Copy Art for Quilters by Nancy J. Martin
A Dozen Variables by Marsha McCloskey and
     Nancy J. Martin
Even More by Trudie Hughes
Feathered Star Quilts by Marsha McCloskey
Feathered Star Sampler by Marsha McCloskey
Happy Endings—Finishing the Edges of Your Quilt
     by Mimi Dietrich
Holiday Happenings by Christal Carter
Lessons in Machine Piecing by Marsha McCloskey
Little By Little: Quilts in Miniature by Mary Hickey
More Template-Free Quiltmaking by Trudie Hughes
My Mother's Quilts: Designs from the Thirties
     by Sara Nephew
Ocean Waves by Marsha McCloskey and
     Nancy J. Martin
One-of-a-Kind Quilts by Judy Hopkins
Pieces of the Past by Nancy J. Martin
Pineapple Passion by Nancy Smith and
     Lynda Milligan
Reflections of Baltimore by Jeana Kimball
Small Quilts by Marsha McCloskey
Stars and Stepping Stones by Marsha McCloskey
Template-Free Quiltmaking by Trudie Hughes
Template-Free Quilts and Borders by Trudie Hughes
Women and Their Quilts by Nancyann Johanson
     Twelker

Bias Square™ tool

For more information, send $2 for a color catalog to
That Patchwork Place, Inc., P.O. Box 118, Bothell,
WA 98041-0118. Many titles are available at your local
quilt shop.